Constitutional Capitalism
and Common Defense

American Political Economy and Grand Strategy for the 21st Century

Cory Newton

0

Contents

This version was updated in March 2017.
Blank pages were added to streamline the flow of
this work. The index was adjusted accordingly and
slightly expanded. 3.17.17

Library of Congress Control Number: 2014914735
CreateSpace Independent Publishing Platform, North
Charleston, SC

Preface

Political Economy and Grand Strategy belong to all Americans. It is time to be objective and think critically. It is time to shift paradigms.

Are you satisfied with the resolution of the Financial Crisis? Are you satisfied with the outcome of the Terrorist War?

Do you expect more benefits than costs to be associated with maintaining the status quo of American political economy?

Do you expect more benefits than costs to be associated with maintaining the status quo of American grand strategy?

Constitutional Capitalism has 3 pillars.

The first pillar consists of the constitutionally authorized interventions into economic activity. The second pillar consists of using the production possibilities frontier to identify tradeoffs and paths to growth. The third pillar consists of the independence and sovereignty of the United States being maximized. These 3 pillars are then checked and balanced against each other to ensure none are sacrificed or compromised for the sake of another.

Common Defense has 3 pillars.

The first pillar consists of the constitutionally authorized provisions of military goods and services, national defense, and international relations. The second pillar consists of the anarchy inherent in the international system identified by Washington and Waltz. The third pillar consists of maximizing the independence, security, and survival of the United States. These 3 pillars are then checked and balanced against each other to ensure none are sacrificed or compromised for the sake of another.

The following pages contain how I think the United States should be run in terms of political economy and grand strategy.

Don't believe that political economy and grand strategy are complicated subjects that you cannot grasp and should shy away from.

Don't believe that political economy and grand strategy are not worth your time, and should be delegated to elites who specialize in these fields.

Constitutional Capitalism breaks down American political economy into its basic elements and reconstructs them in a manner that will benefit the United States in the 21st century. Constitutional Capitalism applies the constitution, to the production possibilities frontier of Economics, which is applied to American independence and sovereignty.

Common Defense breaks down American grand strategy into its basic elements and reconstructs them in a manner that will benefit the United States in the 21st century. Common Defense applies the constitution, to the structural realism of International Relations, which is applied to American independence, security, and survival.

I have not written theoretical abstraction.

This work is a practical and pragmatic foundation for developing domestic and foreign policy implementations that are designed to produce sound policies rooted in sound principles.

Cory Newton
Wawarsing, NY
August 2014

Cory Newton earned an Honorable Discharge for his service in the United States Marine Corps as a Machinegunner from 1996-2000.

Cory earned a Bachelor of Science in Philosophy/Politics/Economics from Eastern Oregon University in 2012.

Cory established Newton Economics, INC. in November 2013. He resides with his wife and 2 daughters in Wawarsing, NY.

You are invited to visit
www.corynewton.com
@corynewton78

List of Abbreviations

PPF- Production Possibilities Frontier

TANF- Temporary Assistance to Needy Families

PFE- Public Finance Economics

NLE- Neo-Liberalism Economics

NLIR-Neo-Liberalism International Relations

NLED- Neo-Liberal Economics Domestic

NLEI- Neo-Liberal Economics International

GDP- Gross Domestic Product
$(C + I + G +(X - M))$ Consumption, Investment, Government, Exports, Imports

GDI- Gross Domestic Income
$(W + R + I + PR)$ Labor Income, Rental Income, Interest income, Profits

BEA- Bureau of Economic Analysis

PCE- Personal Consumption Expenditures

STADC- Short Term Aggregate Demand Curve

MPC- Marginal Propensity to Consume

MPS- Marginal Propensity to Save

STASC- Short Term Aggregate Supply Curve

LTASC- Long Term Aggregate Supply Curve

FOMC- Federal Open Market Committee

USDA- U.S. Department of Agriculture

WWI- World War I

WWII- World War II

NATO- North Atlantic Treaty Organization

IMF- International Monetary Fund

U.N. - United Nations

ANZUS- Australia, New Zealand, United States

WTO- World Trade Organization

WBO- World Bank Group

BRICS- Brazil, Russia, India, China, South Africa

Constitutional Capitalism and Common Defense

American Political Economy and Grand Strategy for the 21st Century

Cory Newton

For Sophie and Natalie

Part 1
The Theory of Constitutional Capitalism
U.S. Political Economy for the 21st Century

INTRO

The Constitution of the United States contains specific provisions that authorize interventions into economic activity. These constitutionally authorized interventions into economic activity can be divided into 3 categories. The first category establishes the general rules of the economic game which include the authorizations for fiscal and monetary policy. The second category establishes the provision of public goods and services. The third category establishes the provision of military goods and services.

These 3 categories of constitutionally authorized economic interventions govern the economy of the United States. The Production Possibilities Frontier (PPF) is an appropriate economic model to illustrate the relationship between the general rules of the game, the provision of public goods and services, and the provision of military goods and services, and the production of capital goods and services, and consumer goods and services, because of the PPF's ability to account for increasing opportunity costs and economic growth.

The integration of the 3 categories of constitutionally authorized economic interventions with an economic model which illustrates the effects of increasing opportunity costs and economic growth is long overdue. The rules of the game are a significant factor in expanding or contracting economic growth. The PPF economic model takes this into account by specifically recognizing how the rules of the game can influence fluctuations in capital stock, resource availability, and technological innovation.

The constitutionally authorized economic interventions combined with the PPF are 2 of the 3 foundational pillars of Constitutional Capitalism. The 3rd pillar of Constitutional Capitalism is the Independence and Sovereignty of the United States. As the economy of the United States is checked by the constitutionally authorized interventions into economic activity, it must also be balanced by whether the economic activity diminishes the independence and sovereignty of the United States. This system of checks and balances between the constitution, capitalism, and American Independence and Sovereignty is called the Theory of Constitutional Capitalism.

Constitutional Capitalism is designed to work in a manner which the economy of the United States is checked by the constitution and balanced by American Independence so that one is not traded off for the sake of another, and none are compromised or sacrificed for the sake of another. This in effect limits the discretionary autonomy of elected officials and policy makers because their constituents will be scrutinizing their activity through the lens of Constitutional Capitalism.

Chapter 1 Constitutional Foundations

Political Economy, considered as a branch of the science of a statesman or legislator, proposes two distinct objects: first, to provide a plentiful revenue or subsistence for the people, or more properly to enable them to provide such a revenue for themselves; and secondly, to supply the state or commonwealth with a revenue sufficient for the public services. It proposes to enrich both the people and the sovereign.
Adam Smith, Wealth of Nations, Introduction, Book 4, 1776

What we all share in common as Americans is our Constitution. There are multiple ways of interpreting the constitution and the multiple subjects covered by the constitution. For the purposes of this work, we shall be focusing exclusively on the constitutionally authorized interventions into economic activity. These constitutionally authorized interventions into economic activity can be classified into 3 categories; The General Rules of the Game, The Provision of Public Goods and Services, and the Provision of Military Goods and Services.

The Constitutional provisions that establish the general rules of the game can be subdivide into 8 categories. These include general economic rules and authorizations for fiscal policy, monetary policy, compensation, regulations on the Executive and Judicial Branch, regulations on the States, decentralization to the States, and the prohibition of slavery. (Appendix 1A)

The Constitutional authority to provide public goods and services establishes the basis for many of the Cabinet level departments and our public institutions including: The Post Office, Department of Transportation, Patent Office, Department of Treasury, Secret Service, as well as departments that regulate commerce, naturalization, and bankruptcies. (Appendix 1B)

The Constitutional authority to provide military goods and services establishes the Department of the Army, Department of the Navy and militias. The use of military goods and services as well as the manner in which they are to be governed, and the general authority to conduct international relations are enshrined in this final category of constitutional provisions. (Appendix 1C)

The mechanisms to pay for the administration of the general rules of the game, the provision of public goods and services, and the provision of military goods and services were established with the authorizations for taxing and spending known as fiscal policy (Appendix 1D). The authorizations to regulate the money supply are known as monetary policy (Appendix 1E).

The structures of fiscal and monetary policy were both significantly adjusted in 1913. The 16th Amendment authorized the income tax which added a major source of revenue to the Federal government. The Federal Reserve Act established the Federal Reserve to become the central bank of the United States.

The federalist structure of the constitution was also significantly adjusted in 1913 with the 17th

Amendment that provided for the direct election of Senators, instead of the State legislatures continuing to appointing them.

A century is an appropriate timeframe to analyze and evaluate the impact of significant structural adjustments to the fiscal and monetary mechanisms which were altered in order to promote the robust commercial exchange and economic growth necessary to administer the general rules of the economic game as well as pay for public goods and services, military goods and services.

The U.S. Constitution is the primary source of law that governs the general rules of the economic game. There are 3 other sources of law that govern the rules of the game which include: statutes and legislation, administrative regulations, and judicial precedence. Statues, administrative regulations, and judicial precedence have provided the economy of the United States with another expense that it is required to pay for called social insurance, in addition to the constitutionally authorized administration of the general rules of the game, public goods and services, and military goods and services.

The broad umbrella of social insurance includes programs such as: Social Security, Medicare, Medicaid, Social Security Disability, Unemployment Insurance, Food Stamps, Temporary Assistance to Needy Families (TANF), and a host of other programs at the Federal, State, and Local levels.

Statutes, administrative regulations, and judicial precedence have established 4 areas under which the economy is regulated in addition to the administration of the general rules of the game. These 4 areas include market failures, externalities, redistribution, and inequality.

Statutes, administrative regulations, and judicial precedence have also increased the scope of fiscal and monetary policy to include actions that promote full employment and price stability, shifting aggregate demand, and shifting aggregate supply.

Chapter 2 Macroeconomic and Public Finance Foundations

The Equity-Efficiency Trade-Off
The choice society must make between the total size of the economic pie and its distribution among individuals

The current Macroeconomic and Public Finance Economics paradigms are unsatisfactory for analyzing the general administration of the rules of the game, the provision of public goods and services, the provision of military goods and services, and the provision of social insurance, in the context of a single model that takes into account the enrichment of "both the people and the sovereign" because these disciplines fail to provide a platform that illustrates the relationship.

An economic model exists which is perfectly suited and capable of providing such an analytical platform yet there has been no formal application of the economic model to the dynamic nature of the entire economy of the United States until now.

The Production Possibilities Frontier (PPF) has been used for illustrating the tradeoffs associated with producing guns and butter, apples and oranges, pizza and hamburgers, even capital goods and consumer goods, yet no one has applied the PPF in a manner which has maximized its full potential.

The full potential of the PPF is maximized when it is applied to the economy of the United States.

The PPF measures output, which is usually limited to 2 broad classes of products, hence the examples of guns and butter, or pizza and hamburgers. The PPF of Constitutional Capitalism maintains the contrast between the 2 classes of products, while expanding each class of products to reflect the actual economy of the United States.

Contemporary Macroeconomics focuses on the use of fiscal policy and monetary policy to control the business cycle. Given the inherent instability of the business cycle, and the idealistic goals attached to the implementation of fiscal and monetary policy, the current Macroeconomic paradigm is unsatisfactory. The measurements of GDP growth, unemployment and inflation used to diagnose the health of the business cycle have significant flaws which make the measurements obtained inaccurate. *(Discussed in Chapter 4)*. The significant Macroeconomic paradigm shift advanced by Constitutional Capitalism, is the use of the Production Possibilities Frontier as a model for measurement of the macro economy, instead of GDP growth, unemployment, and inflation.

Macroeconomic Foundations

The construction of the PPF begins in *Figure 2.1* with the X and Y axes, the productions possibilities curve, and the labeling of the X axis to identify a class of goods and services provided by the government at the Federal, State, and Local levels. *(obviously subtracting military goods and services form the state and local levels, and social insurance from the local level when appropriate)*. *(Appendix 1)*

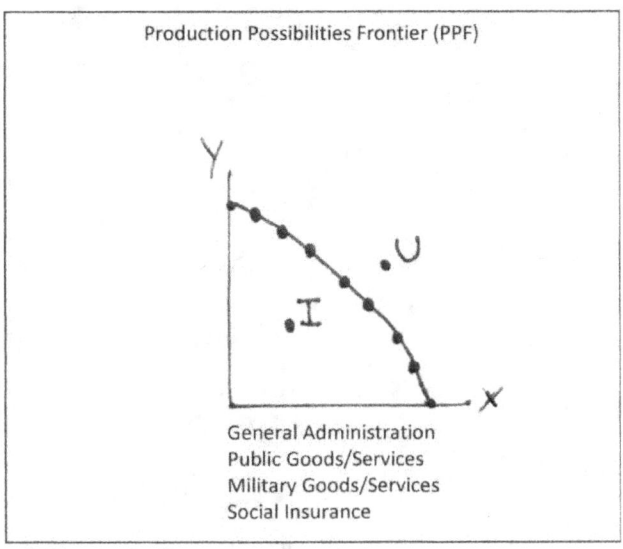

General Administration
Public Goods/Services
Military Goods/Services
Social Insurance

(*Figure 2.1*)

The Federal government spends money to administer the general rules of the economic game, provide public goods and services, provide military goods and services, and provide social insurance, which is clearly reflected on the X axis of the PPF.

In *Figure 2.2,* the construction of the PPF continues with the Y axis being labeled to reflect the other classes of goods and services that exist in the economy and provide the revenue from which the government can pay for its expenses. The government draws its revenue from the production of capital goods and services, and consumer goods and services.

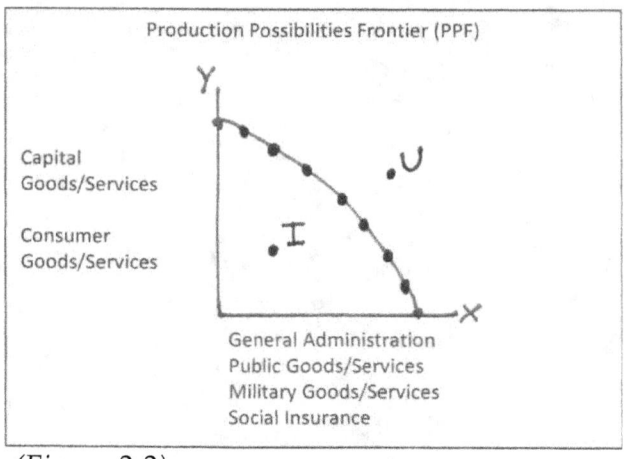

(Figure 2.2)

The PPF will focus on production over the course of 1 year and this fixed period of time can always be adjusted to reflect an increased or decreased time frame. The resources available to the economy obviously fluctuate during the given time period. The technology available in the production of both classes of goods and services may also increase or decrease during the given time period. The rules of the game which include constitutional provisions, statutes, administrative regulations, and judicial precedence may also improve or deteriorate production capabilities during the given time period.

The curve with black points in *Figure 2.2* identifies the possible combinations of the 2 classes of goods and services that can be produced when all of the resources available to the economy during the given time period are used efficiently. The points on the curve closest to the X and Y axis identify the maximum production of one class of goods and services. The point closest to the X axis identifies the production of all public goods and services, while the point closest to the Y axis identifies production of all private goods and services. The efficient use of resources occurs when "there is no change that could increase the production of one good without decreasing the production of another good"[1].

Point I in *Figure 2.2* identifies an inefficient combination of resources. Every point on the curve produces more public and private goods than points that fall inside of the black curve. Inefficient combinations can occur due to a lack of resources, technological setbacks, and deteriorating rules of the game.

Point U in *Figure 2.2* identifies an unattainable combination of resources due to the scarcity associated with resources availability, and technology, as well as prohibitive rules of the game.

The shape of the PPF curve in *Figure 2.2* illustrates the increasing opportunity cost associated with increasing one class of goods and services at the expense of decreasing the other class of goods and services. Each point on the PPF curve represents a tradeoff between the production of more capital goods and services, and consumer goods and services, and the production of less publicly provided goods and services. Each point on the curve also represents an efficient allocation of resources.

"The Law of Increasing Opportunity Costs states: To produce more of one good, a successively larger amount of the other good must be sacrificed[2]."

---

[1] (McEachern, 2009, p. 35)
[2] (McEachern, 2009, p. 36)

The first of the two critical components of the PPF illustrates the law of increasing opportunity costs, the tradeoffs associated with choosing more production of one class of goods over the other class of goods, and the concept of scarcity. The second of the two critical components of the PPF illustrates Economic Growth, which is defined as: "An increase in the economy's ability to produce goods and services; reflected by an outward shift of the economy's production possibilities frontier[3]."

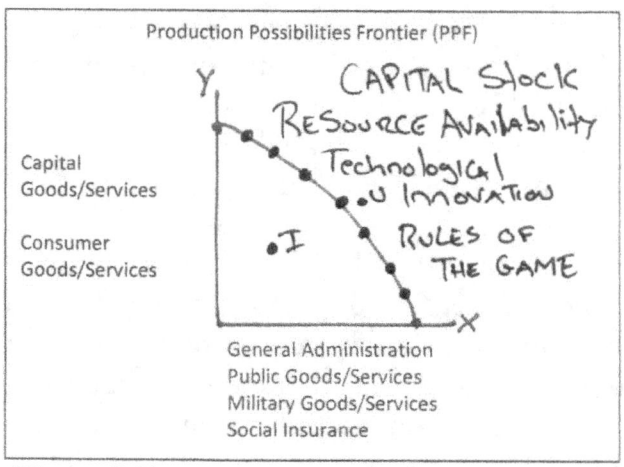

(Figure 2.3)

The factors that can shift the PPF curve outward and to the right and expand the PPF into a condition of economic growth have been added to the PPF in *Figure 2.3*. These factors are increases in capital stock, increases in resource availability, increased technological innovations, and improvements to the rules of the game.

While an increase in capital stock, an increase in resource availability, an increase in technological innovation, and improvements to the rules of the

---

[3] (McEachern, 2009, p. 37)

game, can each individually shift the PPF curve outward and to the right causing an expansion of economic growth on their own, decreases in capital stock, resource availability, technological innovations, and deteriorating rules of the game each have the potential to cause an inward shift of the PPF curve and cause a contraction of economic growth.

Capital stock includes physical capital and human capital. The more capital stock that is produced in a time period, leads to more output being produced in subsequent time periods. In the case of physical capital, if more machines and more tools are produced in a time period, the machines and tools will increase productive output when they are employed in a subsequent time period, which will shift the PPF outward and expand the PPF.

In the case of human capital, if more people are educated or technically trained in a time period, the educated, trained, and experienced units of human capital will increase productive output when they are employed in a subsequent period, which will shift the PPF outward and expand it.

Resource Availability includes the size, health and productivity of the labor force. Resource availability also includes, but is not limited to raw materials, natural resources, agricultural products and energy products. Increases in the availability of these resources will shift the PPF in an expansionary fashion creating economic growth.

Technological Innovations which utilize resources more efficiently and increase productivity have the potential to shift the PPF outward. Technological innovations may be applicable to a limited sector of the economy. Technological innovations have the capability to become a double edged sword depending on the type of advance. Given the "marginal rate of technical substitution" firms may maximize the productivity of a technological advance by substituting units of technological capital for units of labor[4].

The Rules of the Game include constitutional provisions, statutes, administrative regulations, and judicial precedence. Improvements to the rules of the game have the potential to shift the PPF outward and expand economic growth by itself just as increases in capital stock, resource availability, and technological advances share the same PPF expanding potential. Given the structure of the rules of the game which establish the mechanisms of fiscal policy and monetary policy in order to fund the provision of public goods occupying the X axis (*Figure 2.3*) from the proceeds and profits of the private goods occupying the Y axis (*Figure 2.3*), **it is clear that improvements to the rules of the game ought to be specifically designed to increase capital stock, increase resource availability, and advance technological innovation simultaneously.**

---

[4] (McEachern, 2009, p. 170)

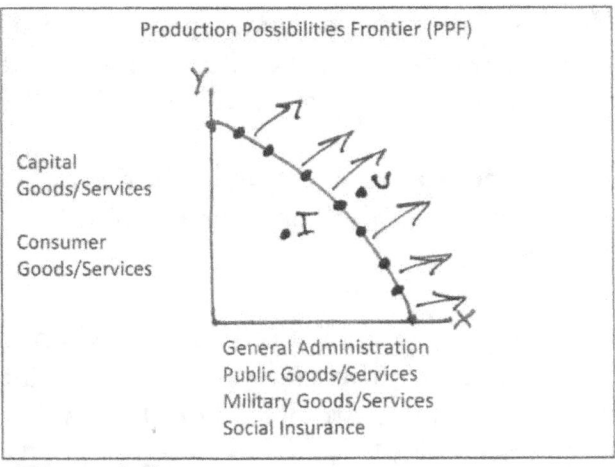

(*Figure 2.4*)

    Figure 2.4 illustrates the potential PPF expansion outward and to the right which would occur by specifically improving the rules of the game in order to increase capital stock, resource availability, and technological innovation. With each of the four factors of the growth component of the PPF having the potential to expand the PPF on its own, it is reasonable to suggest improving the rules of the game in a coordinated manner to specifically increase capital stock, increase resource availability and increase technological innovation.

    Although scarcity, tradeoffs, and increasing opportunity costs still exist between choosing more private goods than public goods or *vice versa*, during such a period of PPF expansionism and economic growth, it is clear given the conduct of fiscal and monetary policy over the last century all four factors of the economic expansion component of the PPF need to be expanded in order for the production of private goods to pay for the exponential growth in both cost and debt of the public goods.

The fundamental economic question for the United States in the early 21st century is: what rate of exponential economic growth is needed by the class of private goods on the Y axis *(Figure 2.4)* to offset the exponential rate of growth in debt and costs of the class of public goods on the X axis *(Figure 2.4)?*

The utility of the PPF is maximized when the class of public goods authorized in the United States by the rules of the game, are placed on the X axis and the class of private goods which exist out of need and unlimited want are placed on the Y axis *(Figure 2.3)*. The production of this PPF clearly illustrates the increasing opportunity cost of producing varying levels of each class of goods and how important the rules of the game are in promoting economic expansion.

Improvements to the rules of the game are an essential element in determining whether economic expansion or contraction occurs. If the rules of the game are configured to promote across the board increases of capital stock, resource availability, and technological innovation in accordance with the constitutionally authorized interventions into economic activity, while not running afoul of American independence and sovereignty, positive policy has been implemented. Expansionary improvements to the rules of the game enable the capital goods/services and consumer goods/services on the Y axis of the PPF to enrich the people and the sovereign.

The foundation of the Macroeconomic paradigm shifting theory of Constitutional Capitalism is established with the PPF *(Figure 2.3)*. It is appropriate to immediately advance the Constitutional Capitalism PPF into another discipline of economics that is long overdue for a paradigm shift which is Public Finance Economics. Public Finance Economics naturally flows from Macroeconomics (*despite Public Finance Economics attempting to wrap itself in the banner of Microeconomics*) and if the Macroeconomic paradigm has shifted, so too must the Public Finance Economic paradigm shift.

Public Finance Foundations

Public Finance Economics focuses on four questions, which in light of the Constitutional Capitalism PPF require revisiting and reexamination. The four questions of Public Finance Economics are:

1. When should the government intervene in the economy?
2. How might the government intervene?
3. What is the effect of those interventions on economic outcomes?
4. Why do governments intervene in the way that they do?[5]

It is important to answer these questions in order and contrast the Public Finance Economic orthodoxy, with the answers given by the Theory of Constitutional Capitalism.

---

[5] (Gruber, 2011, p. 3)

Question 1. When should the government intervene in the economy?

Public Finance answers without citing a single constitutionally authorized intervention into economic activity. In fact, the stated goal of Public Finance Economics is to "understand the proper role of government in the economy[6]". Without a solid constitutional foundation to anchor this understanding of "the proper role of government in the economy", the conclusions and recommendations of Public Finance Economists tend to be arbitrary, subjective, and inaccurate at best.

Public Finance Economics (PFE) cites Market Failures and Redistribution as motivations for government intervention into the economy. Market Failure is defined as a "problem that causes the market economy to deliver an outcome that does not maximize efficiency[7]". Redistribution is defined as "the shifting of resources from some groups in society to others[8]".

The concept of market failure has unfortunately been advanced by economists. When specifically considering market failure related to a suboptimal or inefficient production of a good or service, it is not the market that fails in delivering an outcome that is suboptimal, it is the good or service that fails to clear the market at a market price. If a producer expects more costs than benefits to be associated with producing a good or service, it is a rational economic decision to withhold that production. In effect, the

---

[6] (Gruber, 2011, p. 2)
[7] (Gruber, 2011, p. 3)
[8] (Gruber, 2011, p. 6)

market mechanism works and it is a failure of the good or service to clear the market at a market price.

The U.S. Constitution accounts for the failure of certain goods and services to clear the market at a market price, which is why public goods and services such as post offices and post roads were specifically authorized in the constitution, as well as military goods and services including providing an Army and Navy (Appendix 1B and 1C).

The concept of market failure is broader than the narrow spectrum of goods and services both public and private, and also includes externalities, market power and inequity (inequality).

An externality is defined as "a cost or benefit that affects neither the buyer or seller, but instead affects people not involved in the market transaction[9]".

Market power is defined as "the ability of the firm to raise its price without losing all its customers to rival firms[10]".

Inequity/Inequality are defined as "an instance of injustice or unfairness[11]" and "an unfair situation in which some people have more rights or better opportunities than other people[12]".

Given the dramatic and emotional nature of perceived market failures, policymakers are often encouraged to remedy perceived market failure

---

[9] (McEachern, 2009, p. 491)
[10] (McEachern, 2009, p. 493)
[11] (merriam-webster.com)
[12] (merriam-webster.com)

through statutes, administrative regulations and even judicial precedence. This often leads to the passage of statutes and administrative regulations that attempt to alleviate the negative social impact of perceived market failures by replacing them with government failures funded by redistribution.

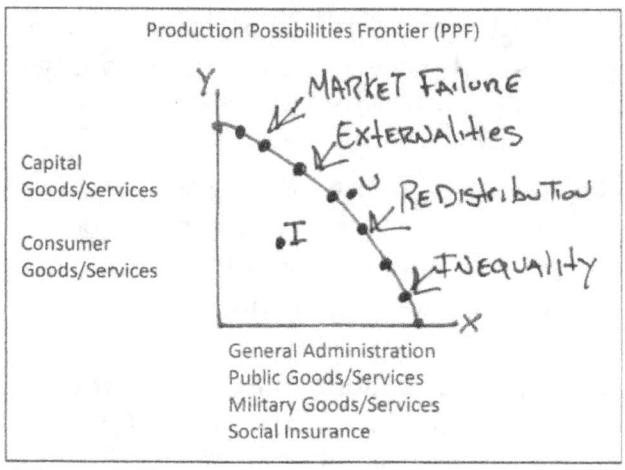

(*Figure 2.5*)

Figure 2.5 clearly illustrates the pressures bearing on the class of goods on the Y axis. The private production of capital goods and services, and consumer goods and services, the proceeds and profits of which are taxed to pay for the classes of public goods and services on the X axis are also subjected to interventions from perceived market failures, externalities, redistribution, and inequality.

The U.S. Constitution accounts for the failure of certain good and services to clear the market at a market price and established certain public goods and services, and military goods and services to be produced publically (Appendix 1B and 1C). The U.S. Constitution also accounted for administering the general rules of the game which provides mechanisms to reduce the negative impact of externalities and market power (Appendix 1A). Statutes, administrative regulations, and judicial precedence at the Federal, State, and Local levels regulate negative environmental and pollution externalities resulting from the production or consumption of a good or service. Statutes, administrative regulations, and judicial precedence at the Federal, State, and Local levels regulate the market power of firms. Some firms are granted monopolies. Market structures are created which allow firms to operate in a system of monopolistic competition or oligopoly. In the case two large firms attempt to merge, there usually are regulators examining the specifics of such a merger.

The concept of redistribution is built into the U.S. Constitution by virtue of the laying and levying of taxes on the class of goods which occupy the Y axis in order to fund the class of goods that occupy the X axis (*Figure 2.5*). The concept of social insurance advances redistribution to a higher level than the U.S. Constitution had specifically authorized, yet through the implementation of statutes, administrative regulations, and judicial precedence social insurance has become entrenched on the X axis (*Figure 2.5*). The Patient Protection and Affordable Care Act is an example of a perceived market failure, being replaced by a government failure, funded by redistribution that was implemented through statute, administrative regulation, and judicial precedence.

Similar to redistribution, inequality is a condition that will always exist. The primary cause of income inequality is the division of labor. The passage of statutes and administrative regulations to minimize income inequality through redistributory social insurance programs may very well satisfy normative emotional or ethical concerns, however does not change the positive fact that inequality will always exist.

Constitutional Capitalism holds that the Federal Government should intervene into the economy when it is constitutionally authorized to do so. These interventions are limited to enforcing the general rules of the game, the general administration of government, the provision of public goods and services, and the provision of military goods and services.

The capital goods/ services and consumer goods/services on the Y axis pay for the constitutionally authorized interventions on the X axis *(Figure 2.5)*. Once an acceptable balance has been struck between the Y axis and X axis that is capable of enriching both the people and the sovereign by creating an atmosphere that encourages the expansion of the PPF, by improving the rules of the game to increase capital stock, resource availability, and technological innovations; it is then proper to address the scope of government intervention to offset the negative impact of perceived market failures, redistribution, inequality, and externalities in a manner that expands the PPF.

Question 2. How might the government intervene?

Public finance accurately describes the methods the government uses to intervene such as: public provision, public financing of private provision, the restriction or mandates of private sales or purchases, and the taxing or subsidizing of private sales or purchases[13].

The answer of PFE economics to the second question is accurate and acceptable. These are the methods by which the government intervenes into economic activity. There is plenty of ground to analyze the scope of these interventions and to what extent the interventions are "necessary and proper". The armed forces and the minting of quarters are examples of public provision. Defense contractors and infrastructure projects are examples of the public financing of private provision. The ban on Cuban cigars and the individual mandate to buy health insurance are examples of the restriction or mandate of private sales or purchases. Taxes on gasoline and tobacco products, along with subsides in the form of tax credits for a wide variety of activities are examples of taxing or subsidizing private sales and purchases.

An important question to ask is "whether the government intervention into economic activity is consistent with the expansion of the PPF"? "Does the intervention improve the rules of the game, by statute, administrative regulation, or judicial precedent in a manner that increases capital stock, resource availability, and technological innovation"? If the answer to these questions are no, then the government is not intervening to expand the PPF. The government is intervening in a manner that will restrict or contract the PPF, while reallocating resources in a manner that shifts along the PPF curve from one efficient allocation point to another, while

---

[13] (Gruber, 2011, p. 7)

altering the distribution of the current pie, instead of seeking to expand it.

The approach to addressing perceived market failures, redistribution, inequalities and externalities ought to have PPF expansionism in accordance with the constitution and American independence as the primary goal. In the cases of redistribution and inequality improvements to the rules of the game, specifically statutes administrative regulations and judicial precedence, that are designed to expand the PPF and grow the size of the pie, will do more to alleviate the problems associated with redistribution and inequality than policy implementations designed to allocate resources in a manner that merely changes points on the PPF and alters the distribution of the pie.

Question 3. What is the effect of those interventions on economic outcomes?

Public finance answers by offering direct and indirect effects of intervention. Direct effects are predictable when people do not change their behavior in response to the intervention, while indirect effects occur because people change their behavior due to the intervention[14].

The predictability of the direct effects related to an economic intervention are difficult to forecast and project. The main error and critical flaw, policymakers and economists make while forecasting and projecting direct effects of economic interventions, is using the *ceteris paribus* (other things constant) economic assumption. The reason

---

[14] (Gruber, 2011, p. 8)

policymakers and economists use the *ceteris paribus* assumption is their attempt to quantify the direct effects of the intervention. When making forecasts and projections policymakers and economists say things like "the tax will increase our revenue" or "the decrease of the tax will decrease our revenue". These types of forecasts and projections hold other things constant in order to quantify, without taking into account the behavioral responses of rational economic decision makers including households and firms.

Rational economic decision makers change the status quo when they expect the benefits to exceed the costs of doing so. In the case of the tax example which holds other things constant in an attempt to quantify direct effects of an economic intervention, the response of household and firms to elasticity's in price and cost is unaccounted for, along with the adjustment period associated with the increase or decrease of taxes. This example is a primary reason many economic interventions are saturated with indirect effects and unintended consequences.

The intentions and motivations driving economic interventions often do not result in satisfactory outcomes. This is due to interventions being based on correcting perceived market failures, redistribution, inequalities, and externalities by allocating resources in a way that merely moves from one efficient point on the PPF to another and alters the distribution of the pie. This method of policy making does not take into account behavior and is severely flawed. The failure to take the behavior of rational decision makers into account minimizes the impact of the direct effects the interventions intended to create, while maximizing the impact of the indirect effects or unintended consequences which are realized after the fact.

The Constitutional Capitalist goal for every constitutionally authorized economic intervention, and every intervention enacted by statute, administrative regulation, and judicial precedence, is the expansion of the PPF in accordance with the constitution and American sovereignty.

Question 4. Why do governments intervene in the way that they do?

Public finance economics defers to the methods and tools of political economy for this question. Political Economy is defined by PFE as "the theory of how the political process produces decisions that affect individuals and the economy[15]". This definition of political economy is unsatisfactory, and Constitutional Capitalism will use Adam Smith's definition which is cited at the beginning of Chapter 1.

The primary reason our government intervenes in the way that it does is because of our 2, 4, and 6 year election cycles which coincidently correspond with the typical 2 – 5 year lifespan of short term aggregate demand curves and short term aggregate supply curves. We will explore these concepts in more depth in Chapter 4. The primary reason the U.S. government responds the way it does is due to election cycles and the lifespan of short term aggregate curves.

---

[15] (Gruber, 2011, p. 10)

It is clear that PFE is disoriented away from PPF expansionism and is preoccupied with market failures, redistribution, along with arbitrary and subjective notions of social efficiency. There are two significant contributions from PFE that are to be noted which include the identification of advantages associated with a flat tax, and more importantly, the concept of the equity-efficiency trade-off.

The equity-efficiency tradeoff is defined as "the choice society must make between the total size of the economic pie and its distribution among individuals[16]". Constitutional Capitalism reduces the equity-efficiency tradeoff down to "the rules of game, and the size of the pie".

Let us recall how the rules of the game and the pressures associated with them lay and levy taxes on the class of private goods and services on the Y axis in order to pay for and fund the public goods and services on the X axis. *(Figure 2.6)*

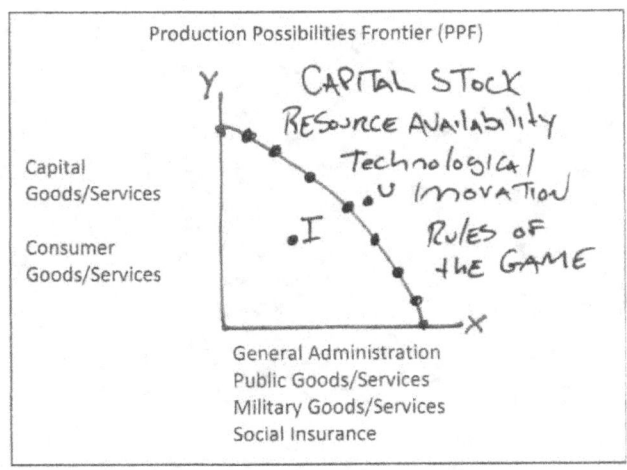

(Figure 2.6)

---

[16] (Gruber, 2011, p. 53)

Recall the added pressure on the PPF from PFE. *(Figure 2.7)*

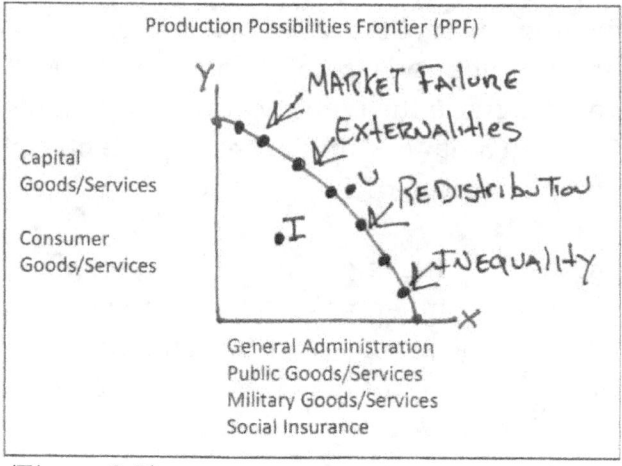

(Figure 2.7)

Are we to suppose, that the PPF or the size of the pie is not to be expanded or grown, *(Figure 2.8/2.9)*

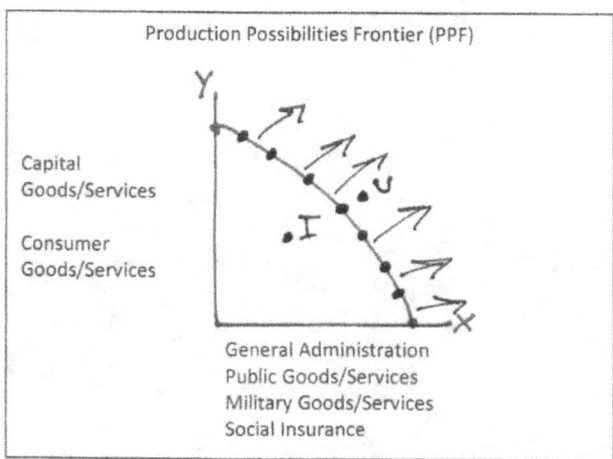

(Figure 2.8)

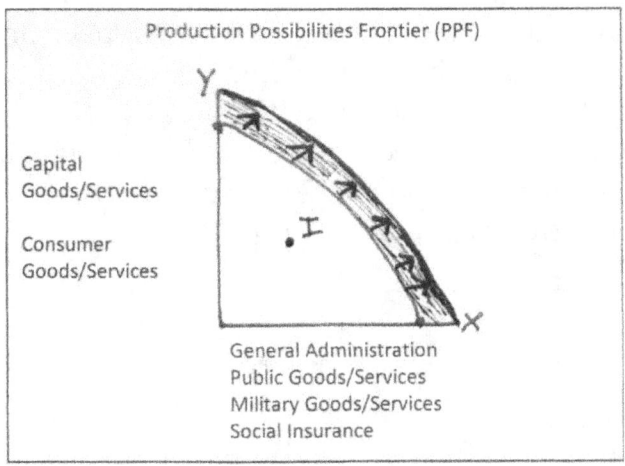

(Figure 2.9)

and instead, should be held constant, redistributed, and divided amongst individuals as if the profits and proceeds of productive output were pieces of pie? *(Figure 2.10)*

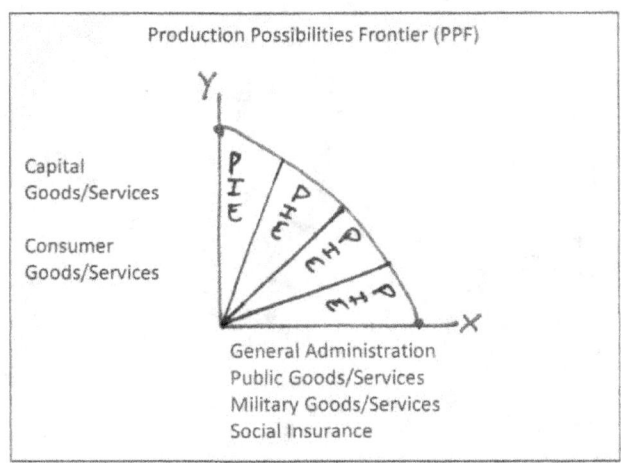

(Figure 2.10)

The Theory of Constitutional Capitalism rejects such notions. Improvements to the rules of the game by itself can expand the PPF. When the rules of the game are improved to specifically increase capital stock, resource availability, and technological innovation, PPF expansionism and economic growth occur. Using the rules of the game to increase the size of the pie is the fundamental Macroeconomic and Public Finance Economic foundation of Constitutional Capitalism. *(Figures 2.11-2.13)*

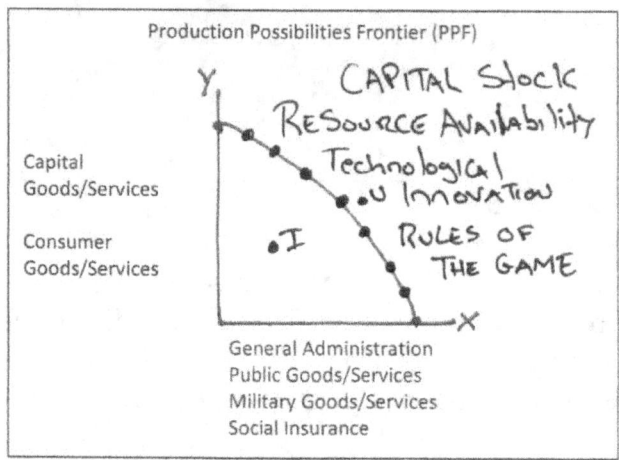

(Figure 2.11)

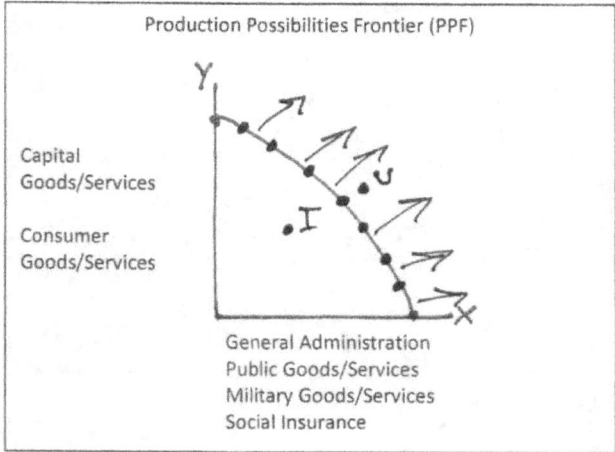

(Figure 2.12)

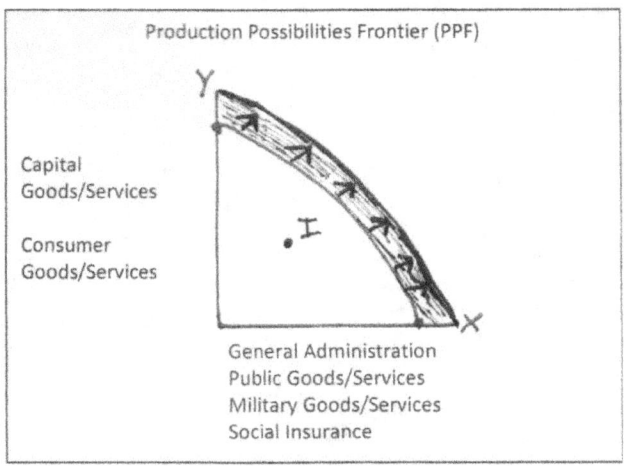

(Figure 2.13)

The PPF expansionism and economic growth resulting from expansion has to be checked by the U.S. Constitution and balanced by American Independence and Sovereignty.

It is reckless to sacrifice the constitution and compromise American Independence and Sovereignty for the sake of robust economic growth.

An equally reckless endeavor would include sacrificing robust economic growth and compromising the Independence and Sovereignty of the United States for the sake of an elastic constitutional interpretation, or idealistic worldview.

Sacrificing robust economic growth, compromising American Independence and Sovereignty, and the sophistic manipulation of the U.S. Constitution, are all occurring simultaneously. The Theory of Constitutional Capitalism has been established to combat them all.

Chapter 3 Independence and Sovereignty Foundations

The Independence and Sovereignty of the United States is the 3rd foundational pillar in the theory of Constitutional Capitalism.

Independence is defined as "freedom from outside control or support, the state of being independent, the time when a country or region gains political freedom from outside control[17]".

Sovereignty is defined as "the legal notion that states are the ultimate authority over their territory and no other actor in the international system has the right to interfere in states' internal affairs[18]".

It is important to clearly state the definitions of Independence and Sovereignty, understand their importance, and apply them as a check and balance to PPF expansionism. *(Figure 3.1)*

---

[17] (merriam-webster.com)
[18] (Ray, 2011, p. 5)

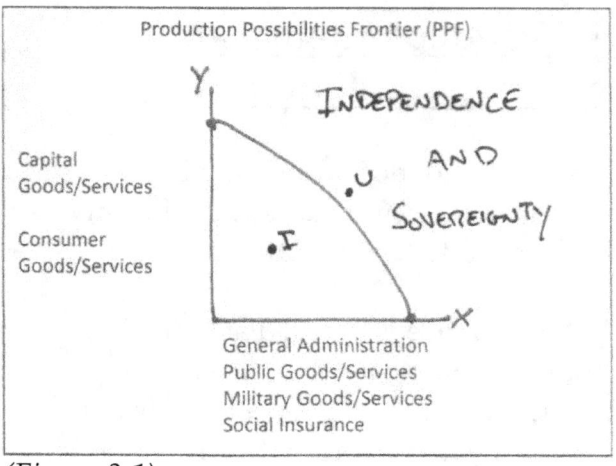

Production Possibilities Frontier (PPF)

Y

INDEPENDENCE AND SOVEREIGNTY

Capital
Goods/Services

Consumer
Goods/Services

• U

• I

X

General Administration
Public Goods/Services
Military Goods/Services
Social Insurance

(Figure 3.1)

The Independence and Sovereignty of the United States shall not be diminished by statues which specifically include international, regional, and bi-lateral economic treaties. The international and regional economic and financial institutions or regimes the United States has subscribed to shall not diminish our independence and sovereignty with administrative regulations.

Constitutional Capitalism will not improve the rules of the game to expand the PPF in a manner that is detrimental to American Independence and Sovereignty. A change to the rules of the game that expands economic growth at the expense of our Independence and Sovereignty is far from an improvement, it is a deterioration of the rules of the game.

There are 3 concepts that require definition, examination, and analysis in order to clearly describe the Independence and Sovereignty pillar of Constitutional Capitalism.

Two varieties of Liberalism exist, one in the sphere of economics, and another in the sphere of international relations. These varieties of liberalism are distinct from the domestic politics of the United States, despite each of the parties actually subscribing to forms of each in some manner. To avoid confusion I will term liberalism in economics, Neo-Liberalism Economics (NLE) and liberalism in international relations, Neo-Liberalism International Relations (NLIR). The third concept to be defined, examined, and analyzed is Mercantilism.

Neo-Liberalism

NLE exists in two forms, one form is found in domestic economic policies (NLED) and the other form is found in international economic policies (NLEI). Ironically the establishments of both domestic political parties contain factions that advance Neo Liberal policies domestically and internationally, while regional factions of each party advance Mercantilist policies.

NLEI became the basis of the Liberal International Economic Order during the "post-WWII attempt to construct international economic relations based on economic liberalism[19]". NLEI advocates free trade to increase efficiency and wealth. Free Trade entails discouraging state imposed penalties and tariffs on international commerce[20].

The Classical economists or Classical liberals such as Adam Smith and David Ricardo advanced

---

[19] (Ray, 2011, p. 357)
[20] (Ray, 2011)

free trade on the basis of the law of comparative advantage.

"*If a foreign country can supply us with a commodity cheaper than we ourselves can make it, better buy it of them with some part of the produce of our own industry, employed in a way in which we have some advantage[21]*".

"*Under a system of perfectly free commerce, each country naturally devotes its capital and labor to such employments as are most beneficial to each......It is this principle which determines that wine shall be made in France and Portugal, that corn shall be grown in America and Poland, and that hardware and other goods shall be manufactured in England[22]*".

The Founder's understood the market and economics. The Founder's anticipated goods and services failing to clear the market at a market price and established a mechanism for providing public goods and services in the constitution (Appendix 1B). The Founder's also anticipated the potential negative impact international free trade could have on the domestic economy, as well as the independence and sovereignty of the United States (Appendix 1A). The power to regulate commerce with foreign nations was established in the constitution to protect industries critical to the independence, security, and survival of the United States.

The United States played a significant role in establishing the Liberal International Economic Order during the last years of World War II. The

---

[21] (Smith, 1776)
[22] (Ricardo, 2007)

Bretton Woods Agreements of 1944 established the
International Monetary Fund, what has become
known as the World Bank, and what has become
known as the World Trade Organization. Each one
of these institutions is rooted in international
economic liberalization, and removing barriers to
trade.

The U.S. economy has grown significantly as a
result of this liberalization and free trade; however
this growth has come at significant costs. The
independence and sovereignty of the United States is
significantly diminished by NLEI. The
manufacturing base in the U.S. which was the source
of millions of middle class careers and jobs has
moved overseas as a result of less expensive labor,
along with governments and populations less
adverse to negative environmental externalities.

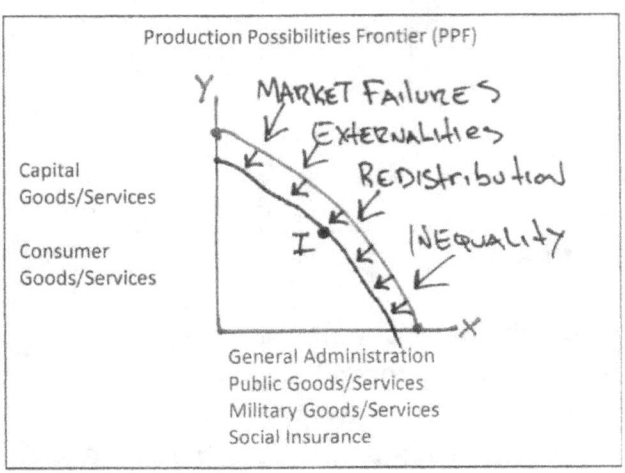

(Figure 3.2)

As we see in (Figure 3.2) the combination of
pressures on the Y axis from funding the X axis,
restrictions rooted in market failures, externalities,
redistribution, and inequality not only restrict PPF
expansionism, but also have the potential to shift the

PPF inward and contract the production possibilities of the U.S..

Producers of capital goods and services, and consumer goods and services that occupy the Y axis are rational economic decision makers. They will change the status quo when they expect the benefits to exceed the costs of doing so. Whether they actively lobby and engage in rent seeking for NLEI policies or simply take advantage of the opportunity when it becomes available, *(Figure 3.3)* illustrates the consequences.

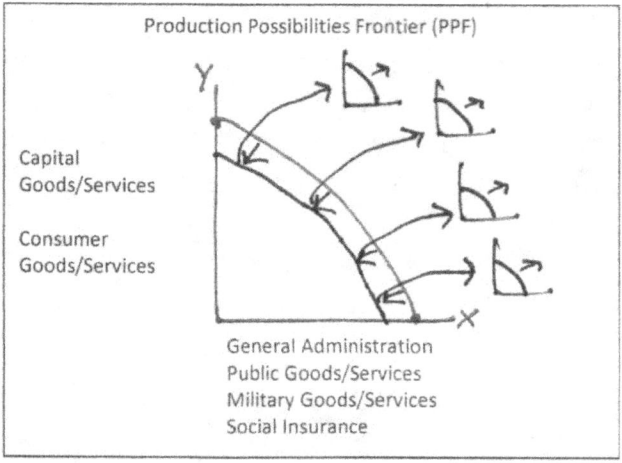

(Figure 3.3)

When the domestic pressure on the Y axis becomes so great that the PPF is about to contract or has already contracted and opportunities become available by changes in the rules of the game, for producers on the Y axis to produce overseas instead of domestically, the factors of productions will flee the domestic PPF. It is a rational economic decision to do so. NLEI changes to the rules of the domestic game encourage increases in capital stock, increases in resource availability, and technological innovations to be produced in smaller emerging markets. This in turn expands the PPF's of the emerging markets and leaves the domestic PPF static or in a worse scenario contracting.

This process cannot be reversed in the sense that the millions of manufacturing jobs and the industrial base that the U.S. has lost its comparative advantage in will not return.
The condition that is truly troublesome and problematic is illustrated in (*Figure 3.4*).

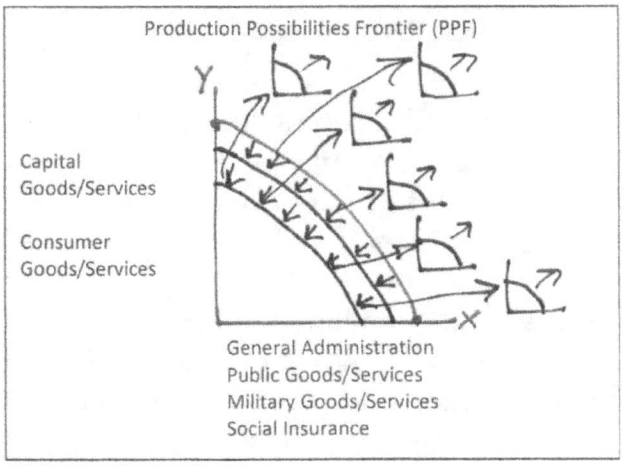

(*Figure 3.4*)

(*Figure 3.4*) Displays continuing pressure on the Y axis, which shifts the domestic PPF further inward in a contractionary manner while effectively exporting increases in capital stock, increases in resource availability, and technological innovations to even more emerging markets with less expensive labor, and even less adversity to negative environmental externalities than the first round of developing countries.

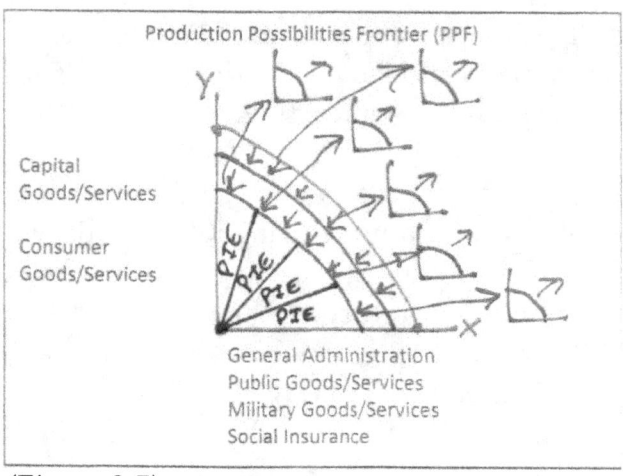

Production Possibilities Frontier (PPF)

Capital
Goods/Services

Consumer
Goods/Services

General Administration
Public Goods/Services
Military Goods/Services
Social Insurance

(Figure 3.5)

(Figure 3.5) Displays the same scenario with the additional pressure of the profits and proceeds from the productive output from the Y axis being redistributed as pie!

A sovereign and independent nation cannot conduct itself in a manner which over burdens the Y axis through statues, administrative regulations, and judicial precedence from the X axis, while simultaneously increasing pressure on the Y axis with market failures, externalities, redistribution, and inequality which are the subject of further statues, administrative regulations, and judicial precedent, during the process of implementing rules of the game which encourage producers on the Y axis to flee, without making any serious effort to improve the rules of the game for the producers that remain to expand. This leaves millions of Americans unemployed, underemployed, receiving various forms of social insurance, and in a state of idleness.

This process does not just occur in a vacuum. The process is part of the Liberal International Economic Order the United States helped establish after WWII resulting from the U.S. subscription to NLEI and NLIR.

NLIR is a worldview that stresses "interdependence between states and substate actors as the key characteristic of the international system[23]". NLIR holds that complex interdependence is the dominant feature of the international system. "Complex interdependence has three specific components: multiple channels, multiple issues, and the decline in the use of and effectiveness of military force[24]".

Complex interdependence is the antithesis of President Washington's sound advice in his farewell address.

"The great rule of conduct for us in regard to foreign nations is, in extending our commercial relations, to have with them as little political connection as possible[25]".

"It is our true policy to steer clear of permanent alliances with any portion of the foreign world so far, I mean, as we are now at liberty to do it, for let me not be understood as capable of patronizing infidelity to existing engagements (I hold the maxim no less applicable to public than to private affairs, that honesty is always the best policy) I repeat it therefore, let those engagements be observed in their genuine sense. But in my opinion it is unnecessary and would be unwise to extend them[26]".

---

[23] (Ray, 2011, p. 7)
[24] (Ray, 2011, p. 9)
[25] (Washington, 1796)
[26] (Washington, 1796)

The United States is bound to complex interdependence by treaty and statute.

George Washington fought on the side of the British Empire during the 7 Years War, and fought against the British Empire during the American Revolution. The British Empire's economic system was mercantilist. Mercantilism is a dirty word. However mercantilism is an umbrella term for many different economic activities. Mercantilism is even longer overdue for a paradigm shift than macroeconomics and public finance economics are.

Mercantilism

Mercantilism is defined as "an economic philosophy that asserts the primacy of the state and protection of the state's economic power[27]". Given the assertions of complex interdependence as prime and the vulnerability of state's economic power it is reasonable to reexamine mercantilism in an attempt to discover concepts relevant to the 21st century.

The fact is mercantilist concepts are alive and well. The trade barriers and devaluation of currency to restrict imports by the Chinese are mercantilist concepts in practice. The Japanese implemented policies that promoted exports and restricted imports through the 1980's and 1990's. Mercantilist sympathizers exist in the United States that raise concerns about large U.S. trade deficits, the importation of goods and services, and the outsourcing of labor and capital[28]". Mercantilist

---

[27] (Ray, 2011, p. 359)
[28] (Grant, 2007)

policies also exists in the United States in the form of agricultural and energy subsidies.

In the United States, opposing political parties contain different regional factions outside of the establishment that each advance different concepts of mercantilism for different reasons. Those who support direct payments by the government to the producers of agricultural crops are accused of supporting protectionism and corporate welfare. Those who support reduced taxes for energy companies are accused of supporting corporate welfare and subsidies.

Some factions that oppose the outsourcing of labor and capital cite human rights and environmental concerns as major sources of opposition. Perhaps these factions are exclusively concerned with human rights and environmental issues and do not oppose the outsourcing of labor and capital for the sake of protecting the state's economic power. They may not even think of themselves as mercantilists, yet are in the mercantilist sphere.

Other American's raise concerns about the safety and health of foreign imports. Produce from Mexico and Latin America, children's toys, infant formula, and seafood from China, have all been put under scrutiny under the lens of safety and health, while quietly and possibly even unknowingly belonging in the mercantilist sphere.

It is necessary to examine the elements of mercantilism that are specifically relevant to the independence and sovereignty foundation constitutional capitalism so the theory is not dismissed as a throwback to an outdated and arcane economic philosophy .

"Economics and politics are related, politics should come first, and economic activity should serve the interests of the state[29]".

Economics and politics are absolutely related in the United States given the specifically authorized constitutional interventions into economic activity. The general rules of the economic game, and the authorizations to provide public goods and services and military goods established by the U.S. Constitution govern the economy. The production of capital goods and services and consumer goods and services existed in the United States before the constitution. **After the ratification of the constitution the profits of the production of capital goods and services, and consumer goods and services became taxable in order for the government to provide general administration over the economic rules of the game, provide public goods and services, and provide military goods and services.** Chronologically, the economy always comes before the state. Once a state is established political economy, the relationship between economics and politics pursues the two distinct objects Adam Smith identified as: the people providing themselves plentiful revenue for their subsistence and supplying the state sufficient revenue for public services[30].

If economic activity is not serving the interests of the United States, if economic activity is diminishing our constitution, if economic activity is

---

[29] (Ray, 2011, p. 359)
[30] (Smith, 1776)

diminishing our independence and sovereignty, and if economic activity is not providing a plentiful revenue for the subsistence of American citizens, then as Americans we have the ability to whistle economic activity out of bounds, and check it with our constitution, and balance it with American independence and sovereignty!

Constitutional Capitalism has provided the constitutional foundation rooted in the authorized interventions into economic activity. Constitutional Capitalism has provided the economic model of PPF expansionism which accounts for increasing opportunity costs and economic growth. Constitutional Capitalism will now provide the concepts from mercantilism that will maximize American independence and sovereignty.

Recall the dilemma presented in *Figure 3.5.*

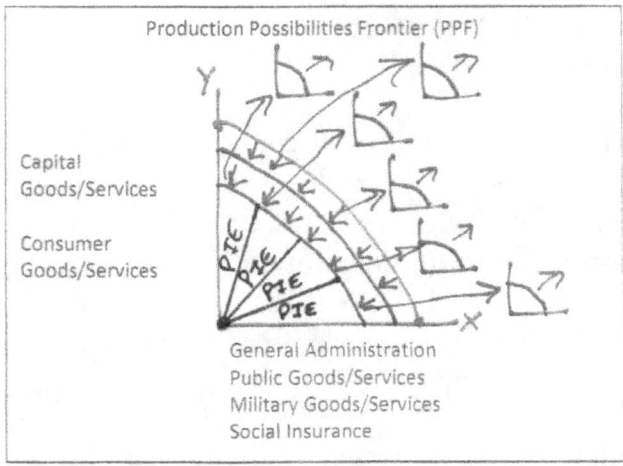

(Figure 3.5 repeat)

Continuing pressure on the Y axis, shifts the domestic PPF further inward in a contractionary manner while effectively exporting increases in capital stock, increases in resource availability, and technological innovations to even more emerging markets with less expensive labor, and even less adversity to negative environmental externalities than the first round of developing countries. Combined with the additional pressure of the profits and proceeds from the productive output from the Y axis being redistributed as pie!

The PPF is the only economic model capable of illustrating problems and solutions because the PPF takes into account changes in the rules of the game. It is through changes in the rules of the game that the dilemma in (*Figure 3.5*) can be illustrated, addressed, and solved.

Improvements to the rules of the game that can secure the economic power of the United States include the following concepts and actions from the mercantilist toolbox:

"Subsidies- Financial aid from governments to domestic industries

Tariffs- Import tax on foreign products

Protectionist Policies- Polices directed to protect the domestic economy from foreign competition

Import Quotas- Limit the number of goods that can be imported into a country

Dumping- Selling products abroad at below cost prices

Balance of Trade- Value of a state's exports minus its imports

Export Platforms- Countries that use incentives to attract foreign investment and production by multinational corporations

Monetary Policy- State decisions on printing, circulating, and otherwise affecting the value of their currency.

Exchange Rates- Values of currencies in relation to each other[31]"

Surely the mere identification of a mercantilist toolbox and description of the tools it contains will make Constitutional Capitalism a target of scrutiny for institutionalized establishment economists in the United States and around the world. The source of conflict and collision between Constitutional Capitalism and institutionalized establishment economists is the polices advanced by these economists have run afoul of the U.S. Constitution, diminished the independence and sovereignty of the United States, and have concentrated increasing pressures on the American production possibilities frontier.

There are industries that are critical to the security, infrastructure, and economy of the United States. Mercantilist tools can be used in an appropriate manner that limits protection to critical industries of national priority, and ensures mercantilist policy levers are clearly in accordance with constitutionally authorized interventions into economic activity, which promotes economic growth through the expansion of the PPF without adding

---

[31] (Ray, 2011, pp. 360-362)

additional pressure to the PPF, and maximizes the independence and sovereignty of the United States.

The United States is suffering from Macroeconomic and Public Finance Economic malpractice that has deteriorated the rules of the game to the point of extended non-expansion of the PPF and even PPF contraction. Since the dogma of market failures, redistribution, inequalities, and externalities is so rigid, rational economic decision makers attempt to maximize their benefits in other ways. Globalization and the Neo-Liberal international economic order of lower barriers to trade enable rational economic decision makers to export increases in capital stock, resource availability, and technological innovation outside of the United States. This has a negative impact on the domestic PPF and the Independence and Sovereignty of the United States.

The combination of Macroeconomic, PFE, NLED and NLEI malpractice has severely diminished the productive capacity of the United States. Serious corrective action is required in order to reestablish a vibrant political economy for the 21st century.

Chapter 4 the Business Cycle and Unsatisfactory Fiscal and Monetary Policy

"A basic purpose of macroeconomic theory is to explain the business cycle- to identify the forces that cause the overall economy to expand or contract. Macro policy tries to control the business cycle, using insights of macro theory[32]".

It is necessary to examine the business cycle in the context of the PPF, in order to drive stakes into the hearts of the prevalent Macroeconomic theories of fiscal and monetary policy.

The three basic measures of macroeconomic performance are Gross Domestic Product (GDP) growth/ output, unemployment, and inflation[33].

Gross Domestic Product VS. Gross Domestic Income

Measuring the business cycle in the context of PPF requires an examination of the GDP calculation. The GDP calculation that will reflect the actual growth of capital stock, resource availability, and technological innovation, is not the expenditure calculation that is widely recognizable as $GDP = (C + I + G + (X - M))$[34].

The GDP calculation that will accurately reflect the expansion or contraction of the PPF based

---

[32] (Schiller, 2009, p. 212)
[33] (Schiller, 2009, p. 212)
[34] Gross Domestic Product = (Consumption + Investment + Government Purchases + (Exports – Imports))

on increases or decreases of capital stock, resource availability, and technological innovation is the GDP income calculation (GDP (I)), also known as Gross Domestic Income GDI. The GDI calculation is $GDI = W + R + I + PR$. Where GNI equals labor income (W), plus rental income (R), plus interest income (I), plus profits (PR)[35].

Jeremy Nalewaik formerly from the Bureau of Economic Analysis (BEA) and currently at the Federal Reserve has extensively examined the accuracy of GDP and GDI. One of many conclusions of Nalewaik's BEA study of 2010 which advocates increasing the prominence of GDI is that "Considerable evidence suggests that the growth rates of GDP (I) better represent the business cycle fluctuations in true output growth than do the growth rates of GDP (E)[36]". "In concept, GDP is equal to GDI. In practice, they differ because they are estimated using different source data and different method[37]".

Given the expenditure calculation of GDP, government transfer payments to social services beneficiaries are not counted in government spending, because (G) measures actual spending on the materials and services the government purchases in order to provide general administration of the rules of the game, public goods and services, and military goods and services. The transfer payments from social insurance programs to beneficiaries are counted in consumption (C) as the transfer payments are spent[38].

---

[35] (econport.org)
[36] (Nalewaik, 2010, p. 28)
[37] (Bureau of Economic Analysis)
[38] (Schiller, 2009, p. 259)

Another element of the expenditure calculation of GDP which adds to its inaccuracy is consumption (C). The nondurable goods and services element of (C) is especially troublesome and problematic because goods such as food, gasoline, and energy products which are omitted from the consumer price index (CPI) in order to gauge the core rate of inflation are included in the consumption (C) component of the GDP expenditure calculation[39] [40].

In effect the consumption (C) component of the GDP expenditure calculation is overstated twice. First, consumption (C) includes government transfer payments which were redistributed from the private sector in the first place. Secondly, consumption (C) includes food and energy spending which is not included in CPI (core inflation). More importantly, food and energy spending is not included in the implicit price deflator for GDP which reconciles nominal and real GDP for inflation. Food and energy prices are also excluded from personal consumption expenditures (PCE)[41].

Consumption cannot occur without production. It is the measurement of production that will accurately reflect the activity occurring within the business cycle. The PPF measured by GDI and other measures of production discussed in Chapter 6, are key elements of Constitutional Capitalism's Macroeconomic paradigm shift.

---

[39] (Schiller, 2009, p. 35)
[40] (Silfer, 1992, p. 115)
[41] (Federal Reserve Bank of St. Louis)

Before we proceed any further it is necessary to return to the beginning of the chapter and recall *__Macro policy tries to control the business cycle, using insights of macro theory.__*

If the insights of macro policy cannot even accurately measure the business cycle it seeks to control, it is reasonable to expect their recommendations for fiscal and monetary implementations are equally flawed, and will cause disco-ordination in the business cycle and disco-ordination in the PPF due to inaccurate readings and flawed assumptions associated with the business cycle and economic activity in general.

Unemployment

Unemployment is another basic measure of the business cycle that must be examined and its components defined.

"Labor Force- All persons over 16 who are either working for pay, or actually seeking paid employment.

Unemployment Rate- The proportion of the labor force that is unemployed.

Unemployed- The inability of labor force participants to find jobs[42]".

The labor force participation rate is another important number that is calculated by dividing the labor force by the adult population and multiplying by 100. (Labor force / adult population) X 100 [43].

---

[42] (Schiller, 2009, pp. 217-8)
[43] (California State University, Northridge)

In 2014 the U.S. has the same 63% labor force participation rate we had in 1978.

The population of the U.S. - Jul 1, 1978 222.59 million
The population of the U.S. - Nov 1, 2013 316.99 million [44]

63% of 222,590,000 = 140,231,700
63% 0f 316,990,000 = 199,703,700

199,703,700 – 140,231,700 = 59,472,000

This equals 59,472,000 people entering the labor force over 36 years with a population growth of 94,400,000. 59,472,000 / 36 = 1,652,000 people entering the labor force per year.

The decline in the labor force participation rate from 67.3% in January 2000 to 63% in January 2014 is the most significant drop over the 1948-2014 time period[45]. One may expect that the aging baby boom population retiring from the labor force may contribute to such a drastic decline. The opposite is true, the number of people aged 65-74 participating in the labor force actually increased in 2010[46].

Those with macro insights seeking to control the business cycle that they cannot even accurately measure, are sure having a positive impact on the labor force participation rate , aren't they?

Not all unemployment is equal, and unemployment has 4 distinct categories.

---

[44] (multpl.com)
[45] (Bureau of Labor Statistics)
[46] (Howard, 2013)

Frictional unemployment includes those in between jobs, and those just entering the labor force just out of high school, college, the military or even mother's returning to the labor force after raising their children.

Seasonal unemployment includes those out of work due to weather, climate, or the season in which there work is performed not being optimal for continued productivity.

Structural unemployment includes those who do not have the skills, experience, and talent for the jobs that are available.

Cyclical unemployment includes is the most troublesome category of unemployment because there are not enough jobs available for those who want them.

The Bureau of Labor Statistics does not measure each category of unemployment on a monthly basis. There are 2 reasons why they should.

First, when unemployment is considered high, structural and cyclical unemployment is present. In extended periods high unemployment it is important to identify the sectors experiencing structural and cyclical unemployment. Once these sectors are identified improvements to the rules of the game can be implemented through statutes and administrative regulations to specifically expand the growth potential of these sectors. If the sector is obsolete and no longer competitive in the long term, those who specialize in these occupations will have to utilize their transferable skills to enter a different occupation or make a human capital investment to change specializations. A job is created, or a unit of labor is added when the employer expects the productivity of that unit of labor to earn enough income to pay that workers' wages and earn the firm a profit.

Secondly, some with macro insights believe there is no long run tradeoff between employment and inflation because a natural rate of unemployment exists[47]. The natural rate of unemployment has not been defined satisfactorily. Constitutional Capitalism sets the natural rate of unemployment at the number of labor force participants who are unemployed frictionally and seasonally.   At any given time people are switching jobs, and entering the labor force. At any given time people are unable to work due to seasonal conditions. The frictionally and seasonally unemployed will usually find or return to employment within 3 to 4 months. Since frictional and seasonal unemployment are constantly occurring, it is reasonable to fix the natural rate of unemployment at the rate of labor force participants who are frictionally and seasonally unemployed during a given month, quarter, or year.

Since the natural rate of unemployment has not been empirically established, let's use the long term average rate of full employment which enjoys an unemployment rate in the range of 4-5%. If 4-5% unemployment is the natural rate of unemployment, then levels of unemployment higher than 4-5% indicate unemployment of a structural or cyclical nature. It is then important to track the duration of

---

[47] (Grant, 2007, p. 502)

structural and cyclical unemployment and labor force participation rates in order to determine whether decreases in the unemployment rate are due to the structurally and cyclically unemployed being hired or dropping out of the labor force. Increases in the unemployment rate due to structural and cyclical unemployment may be due to decreases in capital stock, decreases in resource availability, and technological setbacks, which are unrelated to the rules of the game. Political instability, natural disasters, cyber-attacks, and a multitude of other unexpected events can cause a spike in unemployment. In order to expand the PPF it is critically important to identify and measure each category of unemployment on a monthly basis, establish the natural rate of unemployment, and monitor increases of the natural rate.

Inflation

Inflation is another basic measure of the business cycle.

"**Inflation-** An increase in the average price of goods and services.

Deflation- A decrease in the average level of prices of goods and services.

Relative Price- The price of one good on comparison with the price of another good[48]."

For being considered a basic measure of the business cycle inflation is quite complex. There are 3 different views on inflation. The first school of

---

[48] (Schiller, 2009, p. 222)

thought believes a little inflation is good, usually in the range of 1-4 % per year. The second school of thought believes zero inflation is optimal. The third school of thought believes negative inflation or deflation is optimal.

The textbook definition of inflation as previously stated is an increase in the average price of goods and services. There are at least two distinct schools that differ on the source of the increasing prices. One school believes the source of increasing average prices is a result of an expansion of the money supply by the Federal Reserve. The other school believes the source of increasing average prices is related to imbalances that occur in supply and demand at full employment.

The next complexity associated with inflation is the measurement of inflation itself. The Consumer Price Index, the Producer Price Index, and the Implicit GDP deflator all measure inflation, differently. The Consumer Price Index (Core Inflation) does not include food and energy prices due to their volatile nature. The Producer Price Index includes goods but not services. The Implicit GDP Deflator measures the current dollar value of a basket of goods and services against a chained dollar value. Additionally the measurement the Federal Reserve uses to gage inflation is called Personal Consumption Expenditure by the Bureau of Economic Analysis. However, the Federal Reserve terms it the Chain Type Price Index for Personal Consumption Expenditures! The Personal Consumption Expenditure or Chain Type Price Index for Personal Consumption Expenditures uses data form both the Consumer Price Index and Producer price Index. Food and energy prices are also excluded from Personal Consumption Expenditures[49].

Inflation may be a basic measure of the business cycle, but what it actually means, why it occurs, and how it is measured, is in dispute among those with macro insights. This is problematic because inflation is essentially elasticity of price, cost, and value. The failure of economists to identify inflation as a phenomenon of elasticity in prices, costs, and values is absolutely unacceptable. Those institutionalized establishment economists who consistently engage in malpractice against the public using asymmetric information ought to apologize to the hard working American people. Those who attempt to measure the business cycle with inaccurate GDP, unemployment, and inflation statistics and explain it away with their so called macro insights ought to read this chapter and weep while hanging their heads in shame!

The business cycle has been has described as inherently unstable, which is unsurprising due to the chaotic nature of people having a wide variety of needs, unlimited demands, as well as individual choices, preferences, and tastes. Scarcity requires everyone to make tradeoffs and maximize their utility with their available resources. The attempt to control the business cycle with fiscal and monetary policy, essentially attempts to control scarcity, tastes, preferences, choices, needs, and unlimited wants in a manner that uses business cycle measurements such as GDP, unemployment, and inflation that are at the very least just as inherently flawed and unstable as the business cycle itself. Therefore the results of

---

[49] (Federal Reserve Bank of St. Louis)

fiscal policy and monetary policy can be expected to be unsatisfactory in the best case scenario. It is clear that the current Macroeconomic paradigm of fiscal and monetary policy is based on flawed numbers and flawed assumptions which discoordinate the economy.

Unsatisfactory Fiscal Policy

Fiscal policy is simply the use of taxes and government spending to influence the business cycle. There are two major schools of fiscal policy which are two sides to the same Keynesian coin. The first side of the coin is the authentic Keynesian side of the coin who seek to stimulate aggregate demand. The other side of the coin are those who seek a moderate stimulation of aggregate demand while seeking to stimulate aggregate supply significantly. The Supply Siders would probably reject being identified anywhere near a Keynesian coin, however they have not produced fiscal policies that reject the stimulation of short term aggregate curves, so therefore supply siders are the other side of the short term aggregate demand shifting coin, by virtue of the fact they seek to shift the short term aggregate supply curve in a significant manner.

Figure 4.1 illustrates the short term aggregate demand curve.

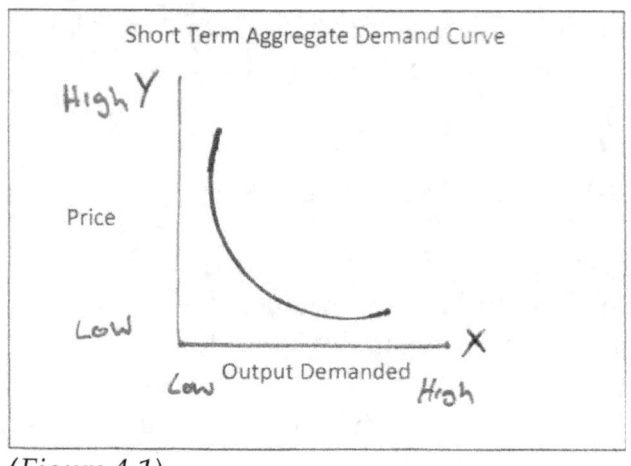

(*Figure 4.1*)

The X axis represents output demanded ranging from low to high and the Y axis represents price levels ranging from low to high. The relationship between the price level and output demanded is illustrated by the curve. When the price level is high, a low level of output is demanded. When the price level is low, a high level of output is demanded.

The short term aggregate demand curve (STADC) reflects the price elasticity of demand, where consumers respond to changes in price with a corresponding increase or decrease in their demand.

The 2 major arguments in favor of using the spending element of fiscal policy to shift the STADC outward and to the right are the marginal propensity to consume, and the multiplier effect.

In the course of the government providing constitutionally authorized public goods and services, and military goods and services, policy makers tend to spend additional money in order to stimulate the STADC. Instead of appropriating money to fulfill the constitutionally authorized provision of goods and services in a manner that expands the PPF, our policy makers attach economic significance to these projects by playing to the donors who fund their elections, and politicize the economic impact of routine expenditures.

The politicization of economic impacts by policy makers increases on more significant appropriations. Let's use a national infrastructure improvement program as an example because Congress is constitutionally authorized to establish Post Offices and Post Roads. Those employed on the project will either spend their income, save their income or a combination of both. The marginal propensity to consume (MPC) is the fraction of each additional dollar of disposable income spent on consumption. The marginal propensity to save (MPS) is the fraction of each additional dollar of disposable income not spent on consumption[50]. If the MPC is .75 and MPS .25 and the amount of additional disposable income to workers on the national infrastructure improvement program increases by $100 billion, $75 billion will spent and $25 billion will be saved according to the MPS and MPS.

The multiplier effect builds on the concepts of the MPS and MPS. The multiplier is defined as the: multiple by which an initial change in aggregate

---

[50] (Schiller, 2009, p. 263)

spending will alter total expenditure after an infinite number of spending cycles[51].

The multiplier effect is calculated as follows:
Multiplier = 1/(1-MPC)
Given an MPC of .75,
Multiplier = 1/(1-.75) = 1/.25 = 4

Given the MPC of .75 associated with the national infrastructure improvement program, and a multiplier of 4, those with macro insights expect the $100 billion increase in workers disposable income, to indirectly yield an additional $300 billion in positive economic impact through increased consumption, for a total increase of $400 billion[52].

The critical flaw of the multiplier effect is that the MPC and MPS of those individuals, firms and households that receive a portion of the $100 billion after it is initially spent by those working on the national infrastructure improvement program are unknown. In fact, the MPC and MPS of every individual, household, and firm varies. It is not even reasonable to expect that those working on the national infrastructure improvement program all have a uniform MPC of .75 and MPS of .25! Since the MPC and MPS of each individual, household, and firm vary, it is wrong to assume that an entire class of government contract workers have a predetermined MPC and MPS for the sake of projecting the multiplier that does not take into account the varying MPC's and MPS's of those who receive income as the government contract workers spend it.

---

[51] (Schiller, 2009, p. 265)
[52] (Schiller, 2009, p. 266)

Taxation is the other element of fiscal policy that needs to be examined in the context of shifting the STADC outward and to the right. Armed with the MPC and multiplier one domestic political party advocates higher tax rates to fund programs such as the hypothetical national infrastructure improvement program, as well as funding social insurance. The redistribution from the producers of capital and consumer goods and services, pays for public goods and services, military goods and services, and social insurance. STADC shifting policy makers fail to account for the opportunity cost the multiplier effect would have had if the money was not redistributed. Despite the multiplier being an absolutely flawed concept, those who are not suffering from intellectual bankruptcy might ask "what would the multiplier be if the money was never redistributed in the first place"? The failure to ask such questions further undermines the credibility and legitimacy of the multiplier effect.

STADC shifting policy makers tax policies reflect their belief in uniform MPS's and the multiplier as evidenced by their support of public works projects and economic benefits of extended unemployment insurance. Unfortunately for one of the domestic political parties they cannot have both ways by on one hand advancing the notion that the business cycle is inherently unstable, and on the other hand advancing the notion that there is uniformity in MPC's and MPS's which result in an accurate multiplier effect which will offset the unstable business cycle!

Flipping to the other side of the coin is the other domestic political party who takes the opposite argument of the taxation element of fiscal policy based on the same principles of MPC and the multiplier with respect to the STADC. The other party argues that low tax rates or tax cuts can stimulate aggregate demand by increasing the disposable income of individuals, households, and firms by not taxing it and spending it in a redistributionary manner to begin with. The other domestic political party seeks to stimulate the STADC with low tax rates and tax cuts while focusing on the shifting the short term aggregate supply curve.

Figure 4.2 illustrates the short term aggregate supply curve.

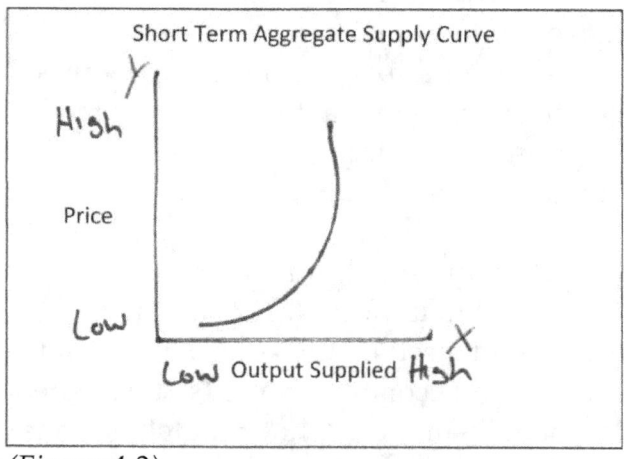

(Figure 4.2)

The X axis represents output supplied ranging from low to high and the Y axis represents price levels ranging from low to high. The relationship between the price level and the output supplied is illustrated by the curve. When the price level is low, a lower level of output is supplied. When the price level is high, a higher level of output is supplied.

The short term aggregate supply curve (STASC) reflects the price elasticity of supply, where suppliers respond to changes in price by corresponding changes in output supplied[53].

The toolbox for shifting the STASC includes tax rates, deregulation, and privatization. Lower tax rates or tax cuts provide producers with a lower cost of doing business, this lower cost for suppliers is expected to result in increased consumption by suppliers in the form of purchasing additional units of labor or additional units of capital to increase production, or to save and invest the proceeds of lower tax rates for future consumption. Deregulation also seeks to stimulate the STASC by lowering the costs and administrative burden of doing business with the expectation suppliers will respond with increased consumption related to productivity or additional savings and investment. Privatization seeks to stimulate the STASC by creating a crowing in effect. When the level of private borrowing and spending decreases, in sectors where government borrowing and spending increases, is known as the crowing out effect. The crowding in effect occurs when government borrowing and spending in a sector decreases, and private borrowing and spending increases[54].

Tax rates are a significant source of political friction between the two parties in the United States. Those seeking to stimulate the STASC using reduced tax rates make the same flawed assumptions about MPC and the multiplier as those who seek to use increased tax rates to stimulate the STADC.

---

[53] (McEachern, 2009, p. 109)
[54] (Schiller, 2009, p. 326)

Deregulation can easily run afoul of the market failure, externality, redistribution, and inequality doctrine of powerful political factions rooted in public finance economics. Deregulation can also easily run afoul of constitutionally authorized economic interventions such as uniform rules of naturalization and uniform laws on the subject of bankruptcies.

Privatization also runs afoul of constitutionally authorized economic interventions, such as calls to privatize the Post Office. In order to privatize the Post Office a constitutional amendment is required. Privatization also runs afoul of common sense in some cases where public services such as the Food and Drug Administration, Center for Disease Control, or Department of Agriculture meat inspections, actually promote the general welfare. There is always plenty of room to debate how effective and efficient these public services are, yet the above mentioned services are legitimate public services.

Unsatisfactory Monetary Policy

Monetary policy is defined as: "A central bank's actions to influence the availability and cost of money and credit, as a means of helping to promote national economic goals. Tools of monetary policy include open market operations, direct lending to depository institutions, and reserve requirements[55]".

The central bank of the United States is the Federal Reserve which conducts American monetary

---

[55] (The Federal Reserve System, 2005, p. 119)

policy. Monetary policy is authorized by the constitution (see Appendix 1E) and several statues establish the goals of the Fed. The primary monetary mission of the Fed is "to promote effectively the goals of maximum employment, stable prices, and moderate long term interest rates[56]". The Fed is essentially tasked with fighting unemployment, fighting inflation, and fighting high long term interest rates. The monetary policy of the United States is similar to fiscal policy in that it is constitutionally authorized to promote public and military goods and services, yet deviates from that primary constitutionally authorized azimuth, toward a secondary trajectory of business cycle intervention.

In addition to the Fed's monetary responsibilities, it also operates as a supervisor and a regulator. The Fed's role in bank supervision involves monitoring, inspecting, and examining banking organizations to assess the condition and the compliance with laws and regulations. The Fed's role in bank regulation includes producing regulations and guidelines which govern the operation, activities, and acquisitions of banking organizations[57].

The monetary policy pursued by the Fed combined with its supervisory and regulatory jurisdiction significantly impacts the business cycle. As with fiscal policy the focus is on shifting STADC and STASC. Additionally, the Fed must take into account the long term aggregate supply curve (LTASC). The shape of the LTASC varies depending on who is drawing it and how it is defined. Each

---

[56] (The Federal Reserve System, 2005, p. 15)
[57] (The Federal Reserve System, 2005, pp. 59-60)

variation of the LTASC has its own implications concerning how to achieve maximum employment and price stability which come into conflict with the other variations.

Figure 4.3 illustrates the 3 major variations of the LTASC.

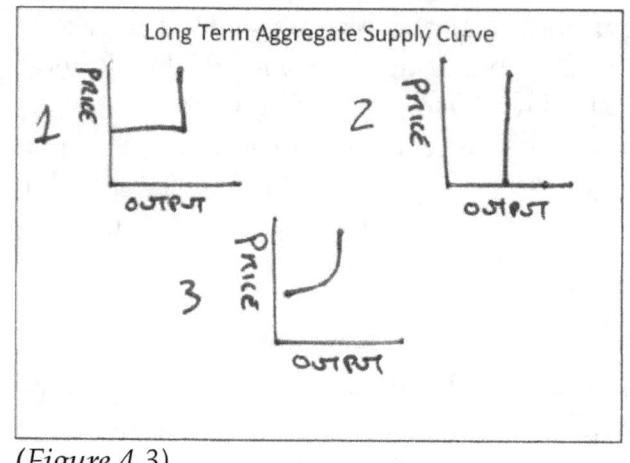

(*Figure 4.3*)

The 1st LTASC marked 1, illustrates the Keynesian LTASC which indicates aggregate demand can shift along the horizontal portion of the curve without inflation. Full employment is reached at the end of the horizontal portion of the curve. As the Keynesian LTASC begins its vertical climb, inflation can occur if aggregate demand shifts onto the vertical portion of the curve due to demand increasing beyond the capacity of output[58].

The 2nd LTASC marked as 2, illustrates the Monetarist LTASC which indicates changes in the money supply effect prices but not output. Monetarists construct the LTASC as a fixed rate of output that corresponds with the natural rate of

[58] (Schiller, 2009, p. 307)

unemployment. Given the vertical nature of the Monetarist LTASC any shift of aggregate demand on the LTASC effects the price while output remains constant[59].

The 3rd LTASC marked as 3, illustrates the eclectic LTASC which is a hybrid of both the Keynesian and Monetarist LTASC's. The eclectic LTASC contains both a horizontal and vertical element which is connected by the upward sloping curve. The results of aggregate demand shifting along the horizontal and vertical portions of the eclectic LTASC are the same as when they shift on the Keynesian and Monetarist portions. The difference occurs along the upward sloping curve where the eclectic LTASC holds that both prices and output are affected by monetary policy[60].

Monetary Policy attempts to shift aggregate demand along a LTASC that's form is highly debatable and contested. Implementing monetary policy designed to shift aggregate demand along a Keynesian LTASC, that turns out to actually be shaped as a Monetarist or eclectic LTASC will absolutely disco-ordinate prices and output. The same is true if the implementation of monetary policy expects to shift aggregate demand assuming the LRASC is eclectic while it is actually Keynesian or Monetarist will result in the same sort of price and output disco-ordination.

The tools of monetary policy include reserve requirements, the discount rate, and open market operations.

---

[59] (Schiller, 2009, p. 307)
[60] (Schiller, 2009, p. 307)

Reserve requirements are set by the Board of Governors "for the amount of certain liabilities that depository institutions must set aside in the form of reserves[61] ". Reserve requirements can be used to expand or contract aggregate demand. If the Fed seeks to implement expansionary monetary policy it can lower reserve requirement which increases the amount of money depository institutions have available to loan. When the Fed seeks to implement contractionary monetary policy it can raise the reserve requirement which decreases the amount of money depository institutions have available to loan[62].

The discount rate is the "interest rate at which an eligible depository institution may borrow funds, typically for a short period, directly from a Federal Reserve Bank[63]". Depository institutions may demand funds to meet reserve requirements. An expansionary policy includes lowering the discount rate and a contractionary policy involves raising the discount rate[64].

Open market operations are "purchases and sales of securities, typically U.S. Treasury securities in the open market, by the Open Market Trading Desk at the Federal Reserve Bank of New York as directed by the Federal Open Market Committee, to influence interest rate[65]". An expansionary open market operation will purchase U.S. Treasury securities which increases the reserves of the

---

[61] (The Federal Reserve System, 2005, p. 123)
[62] (Silfer, 1992, p. 189)
[63] (The Federal Reserve System, 2005, p. 112)
[64] (Silfer, 1992, p. 189)
[65] (The Federal Reserve System, 2005, p. 121)

institutions that sold them. A contractionary open market operation will sell U.S. Treasury securities which will decrease the reserves of the institutions that bought them.

The key indicator of monetary policy is the Federal Funds Rate. "Depository institutions have accounts at their Reserve Banks, and they actively trade balances held in these accounts in the federal funds market at an interest rate known as the federal funds rate[66]".

"A Change in the federal funds rate, or even a change in the expectations about the future level of the federal funds rate, can set off a chain of events that will affect other short term interest rates, longer term interest rates, the foreign exchange value of the dollar, and stock prices. In turn, changes in these variables will affect households' and businesses' spending decisions, thereby affecting growth in aggregate demand in the economy[67]".

What the Federal Reserve is essentially admitting is that a change in the federal funds rate will set off an elasticity phenomenon in price, cost, and value. There is an adjustment period associated with elasticity where rational economic decision makers change the status quo when they expect the benefits to exceed the costs of the change.

Seeking stability in a business cycle that is inherently unstable, using a monetary policy which is fundamentally guesswork at best, given the

---

[66] (The Federal Reserve System, 2005, p. 16)
[67] (The Federal Reserve System, 2005, p. 16)

unsettled nature of the LTASC, is a recipe for volatility.

Chapter 5 Applied Constitutional Capitalism

We have arrived at the point where all of the complex interrelated subject matter of the Theory of Constitutional Capitalism has been broken down into its basic elements. It is time to reconstruct the basic elements into an operating system that is functional and applicable to the current state of political economy in the United States.

The Theory of Constitutional Capitalism will be restated, and then applied to each of the constitutionally authorized interventions into economic activity.

The Theory of Constitutional Capitalism takes the constitutionally authorized interventions into economic activity and applies them to an economic model known as the Production Possibilities Frontier, which illustrates the tradeoff between the production of capital goods and services, and consumer goods and services, whose profits and proceeds are taxed in order to provide revenue for the provision off the general administration of the rules of the game, the provision of public goods and services, the provision of military goods and services, and the provision of social insurance.

Economic growth, as desirable as it is, must be checked by the constitutionally authorized interventions into economic activity that establish the rules of the game, and establish the provision of public goods and services, and military goods and services.

Economic growth must be additionally balanced by the independence and sovereignty of the United States. When economic growth diminishes the independence and sovereignty of the United States, it waters down the very fabric of American liberty, freedom and independence.

The concept of a strong centralized government advanced by Alexander Hamilton has been misinterpreted and abused. A strong centralized government does not administer a welfare state. A strong centralized government can control its borders. A strong centralized government will not allow its economy to become vulnerable to systemic financial risk. A strong centralized government will not allow critical energy resources to be cut off by a 3rd party. A strong centralized government will not maintain artificially low interest rates in order to increase exponential borrowing. The type of strong centralized government advanced by Alexander Hamilton executes the constitutional tasks it is authorized to perform proficiently.

The Theory of Constitutional Capitalism is designed to maximize the benefits of the U.S. Constitution, American Free Market Capitalism, and our Independence and Sovereignty, by checking and balancing each against the other, so none are traded off, sacrificed, or compromised for the sake of another.

The Theory of Constitutional Capitalism is a policy making paradigm that ought to be applied sooner, rather than later. This chapter provides a brief overview of how Constitutional Capitalism can be applied.

Applied Constitutional Capitalism

General Economic Rules of the Game

Article 1
Section 8
To regulate commerce with foreign nations, and among the several states, and with the Indian tribes;

The regulation of commerce with foreign nations has to be rooted in preserving and increasing the independence and sovereignty of the United States while simultaneously increasing economic expansion that is in accordance with the constitution. Policies that do not pass this test must be reviewed, revised, and reformed in order to pass the test. If such policies do not pass they are to be abandoned.

The regulation of commerce among the several states has to be rooted in the expansion of economic activity in a manner that does not diminish constitutionally authorized interventions into economic activity, or U.S. independence and sovereignty. Any such policies which fail this test ought to be rehabilitated in a manner that passes the test or abandoned.

The regulation of commerce with the Indian tribes is a potential avenue of economic expansion that is often over looked. Constitutional Capitalism does not support or advocate free trade policies with foreign nations. In the case of the American Indian Nations, free trade is supported and encouraged to the fullest extent.

To establish a uniform rule of naturalization, and uniform laws on the subject of bankruptcies throughout the United States;

Establishing a uniform rule of naturalization has been problematic in the United States due to the inclination of policy makers to blur the lines between the concepts of immigration and naturalization.

Immigrate- *to enter and usually become established; especially: to come into a country of which one is not a native for permanent residence* [68]

Naturalize- *to confer the rights of a national on; especially: to admit to citizenship*[69]

There is a difference between moving to and living somewhere permanently and becoming a citizen. Immigration does not automatically lead to naturalization, nor should it. Any law on the subjects of immigration and naturalization that does that not establish a uniform law of naturalization is unconstitutional. Offering pathways to citizenship for any group for any reason that deviates from a uniform law of naturalization is unconstitutional and ought to be overturned or abandoned.

Establishing uniform laws in the subject of bankruptcies throughout the United States has also been problematic due to the influence of special interest groups and lobbyists that represents corporate, financial, and consumer protection interests. The bottom line is that the biggest investment bank, the medium sized firm, the small business, the household, and individual shall all be

---

[68] (www.merriam-webster.com)
[69] (www.merriam-webster.com)

subject to the same uniform laws on the subject of bankruptcies. Since each entity varies it is appropriated to establish differing classes of bankruptcies for each, however the concept of systemic risk or any other emergency circumstance manufactured to avoid the application of a uniform law must be immediately abandoned.

Section 9
The migration or importation of such persons as any of the states now existing shall think proper to admit, shall not be prohibited by the Congress prior to the year one thousand eight hundred and eight, but a tax or duty may be imposed on such importation, not exceeding ten dollars for each person.

No tax or duty shall be laid on articles exported from any state.

No preference shall be given by any regulation of commerce or revenue to the ports of one state over those of another: nor shall vessels bound to, or from, one state, be obliged to enter, clear or pay duties in another.

These constitutionally authorized interventions into economic activity have not been problematic in their implementation. The clear cut implementation of these interventions should serve as a model to be emulated by those entrusted to uphold and defend the constitution of the United States.

Article 2
Section 2
He shall have Power, by and with the Advice and Consent of the Senate, to make Treaties, provided two thirds of the Senators present concur;

Treaties whether financial or economic, that diminish the independence and sovereignty of the United States, have to be revised, reviewed, and reformed in a manner that halt the encroachment upon our independence and sovereignty. If such treaties are unable to be reformed in a manner which passes this test, they ought to be abandoned.

Fiscal Policy
Article 1
Section 7
All bills for raising revenue shall originate in the House of Representatives; but the Senate may propose or concur with amendments as on other Bills.

In the recent history of our divided government, the House controlled by one party will pass tax bills and send them to the Senate controlled by another party. In the Senate these bills are completely refigured and sent back to the House, and instead of the Senate voting on the House bill, the House ends up voting on the Senate bill.

This type of policy making is an absolute distortion and manipulation of the clearly defined constitutional process set forth in Article 1 Section 7. It is better that the bill is dropped altogether, than for the bill to advance at all, given the elasticity associated with its origination.

Section 8
The Congress shall have power to lay and collect taxes, duties, imposts and excises, to pay the debts and provide for the common defense and general welfare of the United States; but all duties, imposts and excises shall be uniform throughout the United States;

The power to lay and collect taxes, duties, imposts and excises, on the private production of capital goods and services, and consumer goods and services, to pay the debts and provide for the common defense and general welfare of the United States is best illustrated in the PPF economic model. The above clause establishes redistribution as a method to fund debt, common defense, and general welfare. The so called market failures of public finance economics are accounted for in the constitution, by providing a public mechanism to provide goods and services that fail to clear the market at a market price.

All duties, imposts and excises throughout the United States should be reviewed, revised, and reformed to ensure their uniformity. The adjustments necessary to achieve uniformity should be specifically made with PPF expansionism in mind that is in accordance with the constitution and independence and sovereignty.

There is an endless amount of elasticity associated with general welfare. General welfare is often stretched to the necessary and proper clause and folded to the 16th Amendment and commerce clause creating a sort of constitutional origami which justifies the increasingly restrictive statutes and administrative regulations that justify social insurance programs, increases in public goods and services, increases in the regulation of externalities, increases in redistribution, and increases in the attempts to combat inequality.

Elected policy makers often create this general welfare, necessary and proper, 16th Amendment, commerce clause, constitutional origami argument to justify which ever short term aggregate curve shifting policy, or public finance promotion of social efficiency policy , or international trade deal they are promoting at a particular moment in time.

The Constitutional Capitalist shall be able to identify the critically flawed nature of such policies, and advance viable alternatives to such policies, that reflect a constitutional check, and an independent and sovereign balance upon the expansion of the PPF and economic growth.

To borrow money on the credit of the United States;

Washington's Farewell Address provides the best commentary on multiple constitutional provisions including borrowing money on the credit of the United States.
"As a very important source of strength and security, cherish public credit.

not ungenerously throwing upon posterity the burden which we ourselves ought to bear.

but it is necessary that public opinion should co-operate.

that towards the payment of debts there must be revenue; that to have revenue there must be taxes;

that no taxes can be devised which are not more or less inconvenient and unpleasant;.[70]

Given the $17 trillion dollar national debt, several hundred billion dollar yearly budget deficits, and the monthly trade deficits of tens of billions, which add up to annual trade deficits in the hundreds of billions, Washington's advice from 1796 has been ignored for quite some time.

The government obviously is constitutionally authorized to borrow money on the credit of the United States, yet to what extent they should is a legitimate question which has been answered unsatisfactorily.

The rate of growth in debt and in cost of providing public goods and services, military goods

---

[70] (Washington, 1796, pp. 21-2) "As a very important source of strength and security, cherish public credit. One method of preserving it is to use it as sparingly as possible, avoiding occasions of expense by cultivating peace, but remembering also that timely disbursements to prepare for danger frequently prevent much greater disbursements to repel it, avoiding likewise the accumulation of debt, not only by shunning occasions of expense, but by vigorous exertion in time of peace to discharge the debts which unavoidable wars may have occasioned, not ungenerously throwing upon posterity the burden which we ourselves ought to bear. The execution of these maxims belongs to your representatives, but it is necessary that public opinion should co-operate. To facilitate to them the performance of their duty, it is essential that you should practically bear in mind that towards the payment of debts there must be revenue; that to have revenue there must be taxes; that no taxes can be devised which are not more or less inconvenient and unpleasant; that the intrinsic embarrassment, inseparable from the selection of the proper objects (which is always a choice of difficulties), ought to be a decisive motive for a candid construction of the conduct of the government in making it, and for a spirit of acquiescence in the measures for obtaining revenue, which the public exigencies may at any time dictate."

and services, and social insurance is growing exponentially. In order to offset this rate of exponential growth of cost and debt it is urgent to produce an exponential rate of economic growth that will minimize not only the "inconvenience and unpleasantries" of the taxes, but will also expand the PPF in accordance with the constitution, independence, and sovereignty.

To make all laws which shall be necessary and proper for carrying into execution the foregoing powers, and all other powers vested by this Constitution in the government of the United States, or in any department or officer thereof.

Alexander Hamilton and James Madison specifically addressed the above clause in Federalist 33[71] and Federalist 44[72] respectively. Federalist 33

---

[71] (Hamilton) "But it may be again asked, Who is to judge of the *necessity* and *propriety* of the laws to be passed for executing the powers of the Union? I answer first that this question arises as well and as fully upon the simple grant of those powers as upon the declaratory clause; and I answer in the second place that the national government, like every other, must judge, in the first instance, of the proper exercise of its powers, and its constituents in the last. If the federal government should overpass the just bounds of its authority and make a tyrannical use of its powers, the people, whose creature it is, must appeal to the standard they have formed, and take such measures to redress the injury done to the Constitution as the exigency may suggest and prudence justify. The propriety of a law, in a constitutional light, must always be determined by the nature of the powers upon which it is founded."

[72] (Madison) "If it be asked what is to be the consequence, in case the Congress shall misconstrue this part of the Constitution and exercise powers not warranted by its true meaning, I answer the same as if they should misconstrue or enlarge any other power vested in them; as if the general power had been reduced to particulars, and any one of these were to be violated; the same, in short, as if the State legislatures should violate their respective constitutional authorities.

and 44 were both written in January of 1788 and anticipated that the necessary and proper clause would be used and abused in a manner which would have to ultimately be rectified by the people.

This is the primary reason the Theory of Constitutional Capitalism is a critical paradigm for the American people to use against the current macroeconomic paradigms of short term aggregate curve shifting using fiscal and monetary policy, the current public finance economics paradigm of market failures, externalities, redistribution, and inequalities, and the current neoliberal domestic and international paradigms of removing trade barriers, and promoting complex interdependence which diminish our Federal system, our free markets and our independence and sovereignty.

Every American should ask themselves "to what extent is the proposed policy necessary?" and "to what extent is the proposed policy proper?"

Section 9
No money shall be drawn from the treasury, but in consequence of appropriations made by law; and a regular statement and account of receipts and expenditures of all public money shall be published from time to time.

It is unconstitutional to draw money from the Treasury that is not appropriated by law. If there are cases in which money has been drawn from the

---

In the first instance, the success of the usurpation will depend on the executive and judiciary departments, which are to expound and give effect to the legislative acts; and in the last resort a remedy must be obtained from the people who can, by the election of more faithful representatives, annul the acts of the usurpers."

Treasury without the proper appropriation those drawing the money shall be subject to investigation and prosecution.

It is unconstitutional for receipts and expenditures of all public money not to be published from time to time in regular statements of account. If there is public money that is not being accounted for in this constitutionally authorized manner, it needs to be corrected immediately and this unconstitutional crime shall be investigated and prosecuted if so warranted.

Section 10
No state shall, without the consent of the Congress, lay any imposts or duties on imports or exports, except what may be absolutely necessary for executing it's inspection laws: and the net produce of all duties and imposts, laid by any state on imports or exports, shall be for the use of the treasury of the United States; and all such laws shall be subject to the revision and control of the Congress.

No state shall, without the consent of Congress, lay any duty of tonnage

The clauses of Section 10 are another highlight and sterling example of the clear cut proper implementation of constitutionally authorized interventions into economic activity that ought to be emulated.

Article 6
All debts contracted and engagements entered into, before the adoption of this Constitution, shall be as valid against the United States under this Constitution, as under the Confederation.

This article assumed the debts of the Confederation and established the credit of the United States.

14th Amendment Section 4

The validity of the public debt of the United States, authorized by law, including debts incurred for payment of pensions and bounties for services in suppressing insurrection or rebellion, shall not be questioned. But neither the United States nor any state shall assume or pay any debt or obligation incurred in aid of insurrection or rebellion against the United States, or any claim for the loss or emancipation of any slave; but all such debts, obligations and claims shall be held illegal and void.

The 4th section of the 14th Amendment addresses the economic and financial aspects facing the Union after the Civil War. The Union assumed responsibility for its costs and debts of fighting the Civil War, while voiding itself of the responsibility of to pay Confederate debts and making it illegal to do so.

16th Amendment

The Congress shall have power to lay and collect taxes on incomes, from whatever source derived, without apportionment among the several states, and without regard to any census or enumeration.

The income tax was established by the 16th Amendment in 1913 and has become the primary source of U.S. government revenue.

If there is going to be a tax on income it ought to be proportional instead of progressive. A proportional flat tax on income would seriously diminish the tendency of policy makers to shift STADC and STASC. A proportional flat income tax would be best suited for expansion of the PPF in accordance with constitutional checks and nationalistic balances.

"The fundamental issue in designing tax policy is the equity-efficiency tradeoff[73]". Since tax policy is fundamentally rooted in the rules of the game and the size of the pie, it is critical that the rules of the game are oriented towards the long term growth of the pie.

Obviously the details of a national proportional flat tax on income will have to be methodically produced; however the general principals and concepts associated with a national proportional flat income tax ought to be advanced immediately.

Efficiency gains from having one flat rate on a broad definition of income

The closure of loopholes

An exemption of the poor and low income wage earners

Savings and capital gains are to be excluded in order to promote PPF expansion

Simplicity of compliance[74]

Generous and refundable exemptions

---

[73] (Gruber, 2011, p. 616)
[74] (Gruber, 2011, p. 764)

Elimination of double taxation

Social Security benefits would not be taxed

Elimination of the death tax[75]

The general principles and concepts associated with a proportional flat corporate tax include:

Corporate profits taxed at flat rate

Eliminate depreciation through the expensing investments

The closure of loopholes

Interest deductions eliminated[76]

The establishment of a proportional flat tax would be a significant adjustment to the rules of the game that would increase capital stock, increase resource availability, increase technological innovation simultaneously, shifting the PPF outward and to the right, creating robust economic growth and commercial exchange need to produce an exponential rate of growth.

The Theory of Constitutional Capitalism rejects the use of fiscal policy to shift short term aggregate demand curves.

---

[75] (Forbes, 2005, pp. 60-6)
[76] (Forbes, 2005, pp. 66-8)

The Theory of Constitutional Capitalism rejects the use of fiscal policy to shift short term aggregate supply curves.

Monetary Policy
Article 1
Section 8
To pay the debts and provide for the common defense and general welfare of the United States

The national debt is composed of debt held by the public and by debt held by U.S. government accounts. The total debt (U.S. Treasury Securities) held by the public at the end of 2012 was $11.3 trillion. This $11.3 trillion is broken down into several groups that include State and local governments, the Federal Reserve, private domestic investors, and international investors. The total debt (U.S. Treasury Securities) held by U.S. Government Accounts totaled $4.8 trillion at the end of 2012. This $4.8 trillion is broken down into several groups that include Medicare trust funds, other programs and trust funds, military retirement and health care funds, civil service retirement and disability funds, and social security trust funds[77].

At the end of 2012 the U.S. government had $16.1 trillion of U.S. Treasury Securities outstanding. As President Washington said in his farewell address of 1796, *"that towards the payment of debts there must be revenue; that to have revenue there must be taxes; that no taxes can be devised which are not more or less inconvenient and unpleasant"*.

---

[77] (Government Accountability Office)

To borrow money on the credit of the United States;

Given the open market operations of the Federal Reserve, the Fed plays a significant role in purchasing Treasury Securities which is fundamentally a purchase of U.S. debt.

Is the level of debt that the Federal Government of the United States owes to the Federal Reserve necessary and proper?

Despite the net earnings of the Fed being turned over to the Treasury[78], is it appropriate for so much U.S. Treasury Security debt to be outstanding?

As of April 2014 the Federal Reserve holds $2.3 trillion in U.S. Treasury Securities[79].

As of January 2014 foreign holdings of U.S. Treasury Securities total $5.8 trillion, with the major holders including China and Japan at $1.2 trillion each[80].

Caribbean banking centers and oil exporting countries are holding an additional $539.7 billion in U.S. Treasury Securities[81].

To coin money, regulate the value thereof, and of foreign coin, and fix the standard of weights and measures;

The U.S. Mint consists of 6 facilities including the headquarters in Washington D.C., the depository

---

[78] (The Federal Reserve System, 2005, p. 11)
[79] (Federal Reserve Statistical Release H.4.1)
[80] (U.S. Treasury Resource Center)
[81] (U.S. Treasury Resource Center)

at Fort Knox, and coin minting facilities in Philadelphia, Denver, San Francisco, and West Point[82]. Coin is issued by the U.S. Treasury and paper currency is issued by the Federal Reserve[83].

Each of the 12 Federal Reserve Banks are authorized to issue currency. The currency is printed by the Bureau of Engraving and Printing and the design is approved by the Secretary of the Treasury. The Federal Reserve Banks issue paper currency through depository institutions[84].

The regulation of the value of U.S. coin and currency and foreign coin and currency is determined by the interest rate.

The Federalist Papers are surprisingly quiet on the issue. Madison warns against "a rage for paper money, for an abolition of debts, for an equal division of property, or for any other improper or wicked project[85]" in Federalist 10. Madison writes in Federalist 42 about the problems associated with allowing states to regulate the value of foreign coin[86].

---

[82] (U.S. Mint)

[83] (The Federal Reserve System, 2005, p. 86)

[84] (The Federal Reserve System, 2005, pp. 85-6)

[85] (Madison, http://teachingamericanhistory.org/library/document/federalist-no-10/)

[86] (Madison, http://teachingamericanhistory.org/library/document/federalist-no-42/)All that need be remarked on the power to coin money, regulate the value thereof, and of foreign coin, is that by providing for this last case, the Constitution has supplied a material omission in the Articles of Confederation. The authority of the existing Congress is restrained to the regulation of coin *struck* by their own authority, or that of the respective States. It must be seen at once that the proposed uniformity in the *value* of the current coin might be destroyed by

In Federalist 44 Madison describes the problems associated with allowing states to coin money and regulate the value of it[87].

The argument for a national bank or central bank was made by Alexander Hamilton. Hamilton also argued for a sound but flexible currency.

"The emitting of paper money by the authority of the government is wisely prohibited to the individual States by the National Constitution; and the spirit of that prohibition ought not to be disregarded by the Government of the United States. Though paper emissions under a general authority, might have some advantages not applicable, and be free from some disadvantages which are applicable, to the like emissions of the States, separately, yet they are of a nature so liable to abuse-and, it may even be affirmed, so certain of being abused,-that the wisdom of the government will be shown in never trusting itself with the use of so seducing and dangerous an expedient. In times of tranquility it might have no ill consequence,-it might even perhaps be managed in a way to be productive of good; but in great and trying

---

subjecting that of foreign coin to the different regulations of the different States.

[87] (Madison, http://teachingamericanhistory.org/library/document/federalist-no-44/) "The right of coining money, which is here taken from the States, was left in their hands by the Confederation as a concurrent right with that of Congress, under an exception in favor of the exclusive right of Congress to regulate the alloy and value. In this instance, also, the new provision is an improvement on the old. Whilst the alloy and value depended on the general authority, a right of coinage in the particular States could have no other effect than to multiply expensive mints and diversify the forms and weights of the circulating pieces. The latter inconveniency defeats one purpose for which the power was originally submitted to the federal head; and as far as the former might prevent an inconvenient remittance of gold and silver to the central mint for recoinage, the end can be as well attained by local mints established under the general authority."

emergencies there is almost a moral certainty of its becoming mischievous. The stamping of paper is an operation so much easier than the laying of taxes, that a government in the practice of paper emissions would rarely fail, in any such emergency, to indulge itself too far in the employment of that resource, to avoid as much as possible, one less auspicious to present popularity. If it should not even be carried so far as to be rendered an absolute bubble, it would at least be likely to be extended to a degree which would occasion an inflated and artificial state of things, incompatible with the regular and prosperous course of the political economy[88]".

"Among other material differences between paper currency, issued by the mere authority of government, and one issued by a bank, payable in coin, is this: That, in the first case, there is no standard to which an appeal can be made, as to the quantity which will only satisfy, or which will surcharge, the circulation; in the last, that standard results from demand. If more should be issued than is necessary, it will return upon the bank. Its emissions, as elsewhere intimated must always be in a compound ratio to the fund and the demand: whence it is evident that there is a limitation in the nature of the thing; while the discretion of the government is the only measure of the extent of the emissions by its own authority[89]".

Hamilton understood the issuance of paper currency by government authority with no backing was "incompatible with the regular and prosperous course of political economy". He also understood that the government would endlessly print paper currency and become severely indebted if given the authority to do so. Hamilton was correct back in 1790 and today we are experiencing what Hamilton

---

[88] (Hamilton, Report on a National Bank, 1790)
[89] (Hamilton, Report on a National Bank, 1790)

warned would be "so certain of being abused,-that the wisdom of the government will be shown in never trusting itself with the use of so seducing and dangerous an expedient".

As the government needs to borrow money it issues Treasury Securities. When a quasi-government agency purchases these securities with fiat dollars we end up with the type of mischievous policies Hamilton warned against.

The fundamental elements of monetary policy are elasticity, the adjustment period to elasticity, and behavior responses to elasticity during the adjustment period. This elasticity has occurred when the value of the U.S. dollar was anchored to gold, as well as now when the value of the U.S. dollar floats. Monetary policy has an elastic effect on price, cost, and value to which households, firms, and the rest of the world respond to.

Judicial precedence authorized the issuance of paper currency with no backing in the United States during the *Legal Tender Cases* of the 1870's -1880's[90]. *Hepburn V. Griswold* 1870 was overturned the following year due to President Grant filling two Supreme Court vacancies with justices sympathetic to the constitutionality of United States notes. The *Hepburn* decision found the 1862 statutes which made U.S. notes legal tender for private debts contracted before the statues unconstitutional on eminent domain and due process clauses of the Fifth Amendment. *Hepburn* was overturned on the grounds of the necessary and proper clause along

---

[90] (Conant, 1974) These cases include *Knox V. Lee* and *Parker V. Davis* 1871, and *Julliard V. Greenman* 1884.

with the fiscal and war powers granted to the United States. In 1884 U.S. notes were upheld by virtue of the necessary and proper clause and fiscal powers, without reliance on war powers[91].

When push comes to shove, fortunately the United States has the option not to commit suicide by *Stare Decisis*. The time has arrived that it is necessary and proper to reestablish a monetary anchor to gold, in order to maximize the independence, sovereignty, production possibilities frontier, as well as preserve the U.S. Constitutional system. As *Hepburn* was overturned out of necessity, so too will the *Legal Tender Cases* be overturned.

To provide for the punishment of counterfeiting the securities and current coin of the United States;

The need to punish counterfeiting is obvious. It is very interesting securities and coin is mentioned, while currency is omitted. While the counterfeiting of currency is punished, the omission of currency from this clause and the previous clause should remind us that the paper currency we use for legal tender today which is issued without backing was not intended.

Section 10
No state shall..... Coin money; emit bills of credit; make anything but gold and silver coin a tender in payment of debts;

The Founders understood the monetary phenomenon of elasticity was volatile enough on the federal level. If the States were authorized to coin

---

[91] (Conant, 1974, pp. 159-161)

money, emit bills of credit, and make their own tender, these added layers of elasticity would diminish commercial exchange.

The Theory of Constitutional Capitalism rejects the use of monetary policy to promote "full employment".

The Theory of Constitutional Capitalism rejects the use of monetary policy to shift short term aggregate curves.

The Theory of Constitutional Capitalism rejects the use of unrestrained Open Market Operations by the Federal Open Market Committee (FOMC).

Public Goods and Services
Article 1
Section 8

To establish post offices and post roads;

The privatization of the Post Office is unconstitutional. Those who advocate privatizing the Post Office can only do so by constitutional amendment. This clause is also the basis of our transportation infrastructure. Post roads turned into superhighways and the interstate system.

To promote the progress of science and useful arts, by securing for limited times to authors and inventors the exclusive right to their respective writings and discoveries;

The U.S. Patent Office executes this constitutional function.

Article 3
Section 1
The judges, both of the supreme and inferior courts, shall hold their offices during good behavior, and shall, at stated times, receive for their services, a compensation, which shall not be diminished during their continuance in office.

The Supreme and inferior courts are established as constitutionally authorized public services.

Section 2
The judicial power shall extend to all cases, in law and equity, arising under this Constitution, the laws of the United States,

The scope of these judicial public services is established.

Public goods and services also include the constitutionally authorized functions that were described under general rules of the game, fiscal and monetary policy such as: coining money, punishing counterfeiting, regulating commerce, a system to oversee uniform laws of naturalization and a system to oversee the uniform bankruptcy laws. Constitutionally authorized public goods and services further include the Treasury which lays and collects taxes, borrows money, and pays the debts of the United States.

As we see, the provision of public goods and services that are constitutionally authorized are very specific and very limited. It is through statutes, administrative regulations, and judicial precedence the United States has exponentially increased what it provides as public goods and services.

Compensation, Regulations on the Judiciary, Executive, and States, Decentralization to the States, and the Prohibition of Slavery

These final classes of constitutionally authorized interventions into economic activity must also be examined and considered. The compensation clauses cover Senators, Representatives, the President, and the Judiciary. The regulation of the Judiciary grants the courts authority in all cases of equity and law under the constitution and laws of the United States. The regulation of the Executive requires the president to give Congress information on the State of the Union, from time to time.

The regulations on the States deny them the power to act in a manner that will create friction, tension, and stress within the federal system. Examples include the prohibition of States to enter treaties, coin money, emit bills of credit, lay imposts or duties on imports or exports, enter into agreements with foreign powers, or engage in war.

Decentralizations to the States are of critical importance and are enshrined in the 9th and 10th Amendments.

9th Amendment
The enumeration in the Constitution, of certain rights, shall not be construed to deny or disparage others retained by the people.

10th Amendment
The powers not delegated to the United States by the Constitution, nor prohibited by it to the states, are reserved to the states respectively, or to the people.

The 9th and 10th Amendments serve as the Constitutional basis to diminish the federal government's role in the provision of social insurance. As social insurance is not constitutionally authorized, and is established through statute, administrative regulations, and judicial precedence, the exponential cost and debt associated with social insurance programs can be deconstructed the same way they were constructed through statute, administrative regulation and judicial precedence. As in the case of our out of control monetary policy and legal tender laws, when push comes to shove, the United States reserves the option not to commit national suicide through *Stare Decisis,* and devolve and decentralize the administration of social insurance programs to the States. Whether the States choose to fund or defund social insurance programs should be left to each State and its citizens.

Finally, we arrive at possibly the most important constitutionally authorized economic interventions ever established, which is the prohibition on slavery.

13th Amendment
Neither slavery nor involuntary servitude, except as a punishment for crime whereof the party shall have been duly convicted, shall exist within the United States, or any place subject to their jurisdiction.

Chapter 6 Conclusion

The Theory of Constitutional Capitalism is composed of the constitutionally authorized interventions into economic activity, that are inserted into the Productions Possibilities Frontier economic model to illustrate the tradeoffs between the production of capital goods and services, consumer goods and services, and the general administration of the economic rules of the game, the production of public goods and services, military goods and services, and the added burden of providing social insurance. The PPF also illustrates the formula of economic growth by the increase of capital stock, resource availability, technological innovation, and improvements to the rules of the game.

Improvements to the rules of the game are the critical component of constitutional capitalism. Constitutional Capitalism establishes a system of checks and balances, to check economic growth by the constitutionally authorized interventions into economic activity and balance economic growth by the Independence and Sovereignty of the United States. It is unacceptable to sacrifice our constitution, Independence, and Sovereignty for the sake of economic growth. It is unacceptable to increase economic growth at the expense of our Independence and Sovereignty. It is unacceptable to diminish economic growth by passing statutes, administrative regulations, and handing down judicial precedence that are not in accordance with constitutionally authorized economic interventions. The Theory of Constitutionally Capitalism establishes a system of checks and balances so neither the constitution, the capitalist system, or the independence and sovereignty of the United States are sacrificed, compromised, or traded off, one for the sake of another.

The contemporary political economy of the United States, is in a severely diminished state due to the sacrifice, compromise, and trading off of Independence and sovereignty for the sake of economic growth. Our political economy is also severely diminished to the trading off of our economic growth, for statutes, administrative regulations, and judicial precedence based on the doctrine of market failures, externalities, redistribution and inequality advanced with minimum connection to constitutionally authorized economic interventions.

The contemporary political economy of the United States is suffering the consequences of 100 years of fiscal and monetary policies rooted in idealistic intentions that have sought to suppress the realistic and natural downside of the business cycle. Constitutional Capitalism advances the idea that we must improve the rules of the game to increase the size of the pie, in a manner that maximizes our Independence and Sovereignty, while simultaneously maximizing the efficiency and effectiveness of general administration, the provision of constitutionally authorized public goods and services, and constitutionally authorized military goods and services.

Social insurance will admittedly suffer fatal collateral damage from this approach; however the provision of social insurance is not constitutionally authorized. Obviously the American people feel strongly about providing a safety net for the most vulnerable among us. Constitutional Capitalism can accommodate these American values in a constitutional manner that recognizes the power to provide social insurance are reserved to the States and the people, because theses powers are not delegated to the federal government by the constitution or prohibited to the states by the 10th Amendment. The Constitutional application of the 10th Amendment, in the administration of social insurance will constitute an improvement to the rules of the game that will increase economic growth through an increase in capital stock, resource availability and technological innovation. The reduction of exponential growth of cost and debt associated with the administration of social insurance at the federal level will increase the financial and economic independence and sovereignty of the United States.

This constitutional check placed on social insurance will have a positive effect on the fiscal policy of the federal government of the United States. The decreased taxes, borrowing and debt associated with the administration of social insurance can be used to increase the efficiency and effectiveness of the general administration of the rules of the game, to repair and update our crumbling infrastructure and enhance the provision of public goods and services, fund the provision of military goods and services which constitute our common defense, pay down our national debt and decrease the amount of income the people spend on taxes. A Constitutional Capitalist will reject using fiscal policy to shift short term aggregate demand or short term aggregate supply curves. A Constitutional Capitalist will reject spending money on the flawed principle of the multiplier effect. A Constitutional Capitalist will appropriate money for the constitutionally authorized general administration, provision of public goods and services, and provision of military goods and services. A proportional flat income tax should be instituted that is constitutionally consistent with the 16th Amendment, expands economic growth through improvements to the rules of the game, and increases the financial and economic independence and sovereignty of the United States.

The benefits gained from constitutionally checking the administration of social insurance and fiscal policy must be applied to checking monetary policy in a manner that increases economic growth and maximizes the independence and sovereignty of the United States. Monetary policy is the most misunderstood economic phenomenon. To understand monetary policy one must understand elasticity. Economists focus on elasticity of price; however there is also elasticity in cost and elasticity in value. Today, monetary policy affects the elasticity of value, cost, and price by changes in the interest rate. In the past when the dollar was anchored to gold, elasticity still occurred in value, cost, and price. So, monetary policy is about elasticity in value, cost and price, the adjustment period associated with elasticity, and the changes in behavior that occur due to elasticity during the adjustment period.

The contemporary monetary policy of the United States diminishes economic growth, our financial independence and sovereignty, as well as our federal system. The United States must adopt a U.S. dollar that is anchored to gold. This transition will be less troublesome and problematic once the administration of social insurance has been devolved to the states, and fiscal policy is reoriented to fund general administration of the rules of the game, public goods and services, and military goods and services utilizing a proportional flat income tax in accordance with the 16th Amendment. A constitutional amendment may even be necessary to achieve the reestablishment of paper currency anchored to gold.

Alexander Hamilton advanced the notion that the United States needed to establish a sound but flexible currency. In other words Hamilton was accounting for the elasticity of money, and could have easily advanced the notion of a sound but elastic currency. What Economics and economists in general have failed to understand and failed to teach is that elasticity in price, cost, and value, is a result of the elasticity of the price, cost and value of the money unit, and the elasticity of the price, cost, and value of the gold backing the money unit. This is why economists say the gold standard cannot and does not work; because economists are prone to the false assumption of *Ceteris Paribus* (other things remain constant). Economists fail to account for simultaneous elasticity based fluctuations of price, cost, and value in both the money unit and the gold backing the money unit. The U.S. dollar will achieve soundness through gold backing and flexibility and elasticity through the fluctuating elasticity of price, cost, and value of both the U.S. dollar and the gold that backs it. A gold backed dollar is an improvement to the rules of the game in accordance with the constitution that will increase economic growth, and maximize the independence and sovereignty of the United States.

A necessary constitutional improvement is a second look at the 17th Amendment. The direct election of Senators potentially turns every Senate race into a national election, with money pouring in from both the supporters of demand side aggregate curve shifting, that do not make moral and ethical judgments on social issues, but do on economic issues, and supporters of supply side curve shifting that do not make moral and ethical judgments on economic issues, but do on social issues. The Senate is composed of members who represent the interests of the national parties, instead of the interests of the people from the States which they were elected. A repeal of the 17th Amendment would increase interest in the composition of the State Legislature who would be appointing Senators to the U.S. Senate.

Constitutional Capitalism views the U.S. Post Office as having great potential for the decentralization, and devolution of centralized federal bureaucracy. Local and regional Post Offices could function in a manner that provides public services from multiple departments including Treasury, Commerce, Labor, etc. The Post Office could potentially keep its current postal structure and add cross functional federal workers to provide these public services at the local and regional level.

The Production Possibilities Frontier economic model is easily modified to suit the economies of the States, Counties, Municipalities, and Towns of the United States (Appendix 1). All that needs to be done is an adjustment of the X axis, to reflect the services offered by States, Counties, Municipalities, and Towns. The subtraction of military goods and services from the X axis, and a change in the title to

119

New York PPF, Ulster County PPF, Village of Ellenville PPF, or Town of Wawarsing PPF will work just fine. The PPF is also an excellent tool to use for trading off government services. A good example would be to replace capital goods and services, and consumer goods and services on the Y axis with general administration and public goods and services. The local PPF would then illustrate the tradeoff between general administration and public goods and services on the Y axis with social insurance on the X axis.

The measurement of the National PPF, as well as State, County, Municipal, and Town PPF's are reliant on data and statistics. A good overall measure of the National PPF is Gross Domestic Income which focuses on production. Each component of economic growth has to be measured independently. Multiple indicators exist for the measurement of capital stock including but not limited to: Industrial Production and Capacity Utilization, The Purchasing Managers Index, The Producers Price Index, the Manufacturers' Shipping, Inventories, and Orders, and Construction Spending. Multiple indicators exist for the measurement of resource availability including but not limited to: Oil and Gas Statistics, Independent Statistics and Analysis from the U.S. Energy Information Administration, The Census of Agriculture, and the USDA Economic Research Service. Multiple indicators of technological innovation exist including but not limited to: National Science Foundation surveys and the research and development satellite account maintained by the Bureau of Economic Analysis.

Other government statistics such as the Unemployment Rate, Consumer Price Index, and Gross Domestic product ought to be modified in ways that reduce political and media manipulation. For example the Unemployment Rate should measure how many people are frictionally, seasonally, structurally, and cyclically unemployed. This information would shed light on the health of the labor market.

The contemporary Political Economy of the United States is in desperate need of constitutional and economic rehabilitation in order to avoid national suicide based on legal positivist notions of *Stare Decisis,* to avoid national suicide and oppressive intergenerational inequity based on the provision of social insurance, to avoid national suicide on the basis of an international economic order that severely diminishes the Independence and Sovereignty of the United States, and to avoid national suicide based on an idealistic obsession with preventing market failures and externalities, by increasing redistribution and reducing inequality.

I have offered the Theory of Constitutional Capitalism as a new paradigm of political economy for the United States in the 21st century to avoid national suicide through critically flawed domestic policy implementations rooted in idealism. If we can avoid national suicide by adopting Constitutional Capitalism as a new paradigm of political economy for domestic policy implementations, then we as American will have a chance to avoid national suicide through the lack of grand strategy and flawed foreign policy implementation rooted in idealism. I will now offer a new paradigm of grand strategy for the United States in the 21st Century to

121

avoid national suicide called the Theory of Common Defense.

Part 2
The Theory of Common Defense
U.S. Grand Strategy for the 21st Century

Intro

The Constitution of the United States contains specific provisions that authorize the Common Defense of the United States. These constitutionally authorized provisions can be divided into 3 categories. The first category establishes the production of military goods and services, the second category establishes the scope of national defense, and the third category establishes the scope of international relations and conduct of Foreign Policy.

These 3 categories of constitutionally authorized provisions govern the production of military goods and services, national defense, and international relations and foreign policy of the United States. In order for the United States to maintain and increase its Independence and Sovereignty it must establish a long term grand strategy that accounts for the anarchy inherent in the international system, the geographical boundaries of the nation, and the nature of warfighting, intelligence, diplomacy, economic globalization, domestic politics and scarcity.

The Theory of Common Defense is a system of checks and balances designed to check the provision of military goods and services, national defense, and international relations of the United States against the Constitution, the Economy, and the Independence and sovereignty of the United States that so none are sacrificed, compromised or traded off for the sake of another.

Constitutional Capitalism and Common Defense are by no means mutually exclusive. Both

126

Constitutional Capitalism and Common Defense ought to be worked towards simultaneously. Momentum gained from strides towards one can be applied toward the other and synergistically be developed into an evolving complementary dynamic system that maximizes American constitutionalism, capitalism, independence, and sovereignty.

Chapter 1 Grand Strategic Formulation

"The entire conduct of warfare and peacetime preparation for war are in turn subordinate expressions of national struggles that unfold at the highest level of grand strategy, where all that is military happens within the much broader context of domestic governance, international politics, economic activity, and their ancillaries."[92]

The grand strategy of the United States should simply be to maximize our Independence and Sovereignty. When the Independence and Sovereignty of the United States are diminished or are under assault, the security and the survival of the United States are also diminished and under assault.

There has been no better advice on the subject of American grand strategy, than the advice given by George Washington in his Farewell Address of 1796. Obviously some will be quick to point out that the world has changed and circumstances have become significantly more complex, and the world has become significantly more dynamic than Washington's world of 1796. I'm going to argue that it hasn't. I'm not going to argue that we need to rigidly implement Washington's advice for the sake of nostalgia; however I'm going to argue that Washington's advice is consistent with the contemporary Structural-Realist worldview that is the main alternative to the dominant Neo-Liberal worldview in modern day international relations.

---

[92] (Luttwak, 1987, p. 70)

It is necessary to examine Washington's advice for implementing American Grand Strategy and apply those principles to the theory of Structural Realism developed by Kenneth Waltz.

"Observe good faith and justice towards all nations; cultivate peace and harmony with all; religion and morality enjoin this conduct, and can it be that good policy does not equally not equally enjoin it?

The great rule of conduct for us, in regard to foreign nations, is, in extending our commercial relations, to have with them as little political connexion as possible. So far as we have already formed engagements, let them be fulfilled with perfect good faith. Here let us stop.

Our detached and distant situation invites and enables us to pursue a different course. If we remain one people, under an efficient government, the period is not far off, when we may defy material injury from external annoyance; when we may take such an attitude as will cause the neutrality, we may at any time resolve upon, to be scrupulously respected; when belligerent nations, under the impossibility of making acquisitions upon us, will not lightly hazard the giving us provocation; when we may choose peace or war, as our interest, guided by justice, shall counsel.

Why forego the advantages of so peculiar a situation? Why quit our own to stand upon foreign ground? Why, by interweaving our destiny with that of any part of Europe, entangle our peace and prosperity in the toils of European ambition, rivalship, interest, humor, or caprice?

It is our true policy to steer clear of permanent alliances with any portion of the foreign world; so far, I mean, as we are now at liberty to do it; for let me not be understood as capable of patronizing infidelity to existing engagements. I hold the maxim no less applicable to public than to private affairs, that honesty is always the best policy. I repeat it, therefore, let those engagements be observed in their genuine sense. But, in my opinion, it is unnecessary and would be unwise to extend them.

Harmony, liberal intercourse with all nations, are recommended by policy, humanity, and interest. But even our commercial policy should hold an equal and impartial hand; neither seeking nor granting exclusive favors or preferences; consulting the natural course of things; diffusing and diversifying by gentle means the streams of commerce, but forcing nothing; establishing, with powers so disposed, in order to give trade a stable course, to define the rights of our merchants, and to enable the government to support them, conventional rules of intercourse, the best that present circumstances and mutual opinion will permit, but temporary, and liable to be from time to time abandoned or varied, as experience and circumstances shall dictate; constantly keeping in view, that it is folly in one nation to look for disinterested favors from another; that it must pay with a portion of its independence for whatever it may accept under that character; that, by such acceptance, it may place itself in the condition of having given equivalents for nominal favors, and yet of being reproached with ingratitude for not giving more. There can be no greater error than to expect or calculate upon real favors from nation to nation. It is an illusion, which experience must cure, which a just pride ought to discard.

The duty of holding a neutral conduct may be inferred, without any thing more, from the obligation which justice and humanity impose on every nation, in cases in which it is free to act, to maintain inviolate the relations of peace and amity towards other nations."[93]

---

[93] (Washington, 1796, pp. 25-35)

There are several themes that Washington repeated and stressed in 1796 that are still very important today in 2014. Washington gave sound timeless advice which would make him a pariah in today's contemporary political parties.

Washington recommended that we observe faith and justice and cultivate peace and harmony with all nations. To do so would require not making moral and ethical judgments. For at least the past 100 years the American international relations and foreign policy establishments have been filled with idealists making moral and ethical judgments on nations.

Washington proclaimed that the great rule of conduct for the United States in regard to foreign nations was to extend our commercial relations while maintaining minimal political connection with them. This runs contrary to the contemporary political calls for improved labor conditions, increased environmental protections, and human rights monitoring routinely called for today.

Washington's then reminds us of our geographic location in relation to the rest of the world and recommends a policy of neutrality to maximize our security, survival, and independence. This policy of neutrality will enable us to choose peace or war based on our interests which are guided by justice. Washington then challenges those who would wave the banner of American morality, ethics, and justice upon foreign ground to explain why our peace and prosperity should be risked for foreign interwoven entanglements overseas.

Given the 4 recommendations of Washington selected so far, the United States has run afoul of all 4 since at least the beginning of our involvement in WWI almost 100 years ago.

The 5th recommendation of Washington to steer clear of permanent alliances with any portion of the foreign world has also gone unheeded. One only needs to examine the U.S. relationships with Great Britain, NATO, Japan, South Korea, and Israel to observe that Washington's advice has been discarded.

The 6th recommendation of Washington stipulated that our commercial policy should hold an equal and impartial hand, neither seeking nor granting exclusive favors or preferences. He further warned that there can be no greater error than to expect or calculate upon real favors from nation to nation. It is an illusion which experience must cure, which a just pride ought to discard.

The reason it is important to examine these recommendations from Washington's Farewell Address is because they are a complete refutation of our current support of and participation in the Neo-Liberal international economic order, and a complete refutation of the collective security agreements, treaties, and alliances we have maintained since the end of WWII.

Obviously if the elites and the masses gave a damn about what Washington said in his Farewell address concerning international commerce, international relations, and grand strategy, his recommendations and our contemporary policy implementations would not occupy different ends of the spectrum. Since his recommendations and our contemporary policy implementations do occupy different ends of the spectrum it is necessary to examine contemporary material that supports the antithesis of our commitment to the Neo-Liberal international order and collective security agreements in order to determine if Washington's advice is indeed outdated and irrelevant in the 21st century.

"A system is composed of a structure and of interacting units[94]". Washington obviously considered nations to be the primary actors in the international system. Washington urges two very different recommended courses of action for two very different systems. The course of action recommend by Washington for the American domestic political system is a recommendation very different from the action he recommends for the international system.

"To the efficacy and permanency of your Union, a Government for the whole is indispensable. No alliances, however strict, between the parts can be an adequate substitute; they must inevitably experience the infractions and interruptions, which all alliances in all times have experienced. Sensible of this momentous truth, you have improved upon your first essay, by the adoption of a Constitution of Government better calculated than your former for an intimate Union, and for the efficacious management of your common concerns. This Government, the offspring of our own choice, uninfluenced and unawed, adopted upon full investigation and mature deliberation, completely free in its principles, in the distribution of its powers, uniting security with energy, and containing within itself a provision for its own amendment, has a just

---

[94] (Waltz, 1979, p. 79)

claim to your confidence and your support. Respect for its authority, compliance with its laws, acquiescence in its measures, are duties enjoined by the fundamental maxims of true Liberty. The basis of our political systems is the right of the people to make and to alter their Constitutions of Government. But the Constitution which at any time exists, till changed by an explicit and authentic act of the whole people, is sacredly obligatory upon all. The very idea of the power and the right of the people to establish Government presupposes the duty of every individual to obey the established Government[95]."

The reason for the two different recommendations from Washington is due to the differences in the ordering principles of the national system and international system. The ordering principles of national systems are hierarchy and centralization while the ordering principles in the international system are anarchy and decentralization[96]. The Constitution of the United States is the hierarchic, centralized ordering principle and structure of the American Federalist system. The units in the American federal system include States, Counties, Municipalities, Towns, and Cabinet level Departments. Each of these units have varying degrees of interdependence amongst each other, while operating and functioning in their respective spheres of influence in a hierarchic structure. "National politics consists of differentiated units performing specified functions. International politics consists of like units duplicating one another's activities[97]".

---

[95] (Washington, 1796, pp. 15-6)
[96] (Waltz, 1979, p. 88)
[97] (Waltz, 1979, p. 97)

The first 10 Federalist Papers written from October 27, 1787 – November 22, 1787 argue for Union based on the ordering principles of hierarchy and centralization, in order to fight off foreign influence, establish security, enhance prospects of survival, maintain independence and sovereignty, and reduce the negative impact of factionalism due the centralized and hierarchic structure of the Constitutional system[98].

Washington, Hamilton, Jay, and Madison understood that without a centralized and hierarchic structural ordering system to unify the American States, the States would become units subject to the anarchic, decentralized structure of the international system. Washington, Hamilton, Jay, and Madison understood that "in anarchy, security is the highest end[99]", "survival is a prerequisite to achieving any goals the state might have[100]", and "to say that a state is sovereign means that it decides for itself how it will cope with its internal and external problems, including whether or not to seek assistance from others and in doing so limit its freedom by making commitments to them[101]".

The colonies victory in the revolution required them to unite under a hierarchic, centralized national system in order to achieve security, survival, and sovereignty in the face of the decentralized anarchy of the international system. Washington recommended having minimal political ties, minimal commitments, and pursuing a course of neutrality with foreign nations because not doing so would

---

[98] (Hamilton M. J., 1787, pp. 1-10)
[99] (Waltz, 1979, p. 126)
[100] (Waltz, 1979, p. 91)
[101] (Waltz, 1979, p. 96)

reduce the freedom and independence of young America, which in turn could threaten America's security, survival, and sovereignty.

It is necessary to examine if the structure of the international system, and the international systems itself has changed since 1776-1796 in order to determine if it is sound and timely to implement policies that are the polar opposite of the recommendations from Washington's farewell address with respect to our interaction with units in the international system.

The modern international system in which the state became a sovereign unit in the anarchic structure of the international system began at the Peace of Westphalia that ended The Thirty Years War in 1648. Multi-polarity was the way of the world and of the international system from 1648 until 1945 (meaning several powerful states dominated the international system).

Some of these states and empires included: France, Venice, the Qing Empire, the Safavid Empire, the Dutch Empire, the British Empire, the Mughal Empire, the Ottoman Empire, the Polish-Lithuanian Commonwealth, Portugal, Prussia, the Spanish Empire, Sweden, the Russian Empire, the Persian Empire, the Austrian Empire, the Italian Empire, the Japanese Empire, Nazi Germany, the Soviet Union, and the United States[102][103]. The period from 1648 to 1945 spanned 297 years. During these 297 years there were 21 major states/empires that rose, fell, morphed, or transformed.

---

[102] (List of pre-modern great powers)
[103] (List of great powers by date)

From 1945 until 1991 bi-polarity (meaning two powerful states dominated the international system) was the way of the world. During this 46 year period the Soviet Union and United States dominated the international system because they were the strongest states to emerge from World War II. The Soviet Union and the United States each created collective security agreements with satellite nations in their spheres of influence. These satellite nations received tremendous material support from the superpowers which they orbited.

From 1991 until 2008 uni-polarity (meaning one powerful state dominated the international system) was the way of the world. In this 17 year period the United States dominated the international system. Due to unipolar overextension which specifically includes nation building and fighting prolonged medium to low intensity counter insurgencies in 3rd world countries, combined with domestic financial and economic overextension specifically including the costs and debt associated with social insurance programs, banking bailouts, and the exponential issuance of Treasury Securities, the multi polar realignment has begun.

Bi-polarity lasted for 46 years. Uni-polarity lasted 17. As the international system has begun to transition back to multi-polarity over the past 6 years it is important for the United States to be prepared to maximize its security, independence, and survival in a multi-polar system. Yet, the United States fails to recognize the writing on the wall. The foreign and domestic policies of the United States are implemented in a manner that speeds the uni-polar overextension of America towards the brink of collapse.

Just as global Marxism failed, the neo-liberal international order of global capitalism, open borders, open markets, and collective security agreements is crumbling before our eyes. It took global Marxism 46 years to fail. It may take the post WWII neo-liberal international order 75 years to fail. That leaves us with 6 years if we are lucky, which will get us to 2020.

1991 would have been a good time to reorient the United States toward a grand strategy of maximizing our security, independence, and survival. This did not occur. Instead of implementing a realistic grand strategy, the United States pursued an idealistic foreign policy. An idealistic foreign policy still pursued today that has failed to meet any of its goals or aims.

Instead of disbanding the collective security agreements and treaty guarantees from the bi-polar era the U.S. has maintained or expanded them. Instead of re-reading Washington's advice from his Farewell Address, a New World Order was proclaimed. The building of a Global Village and Bridge to the 21st Century was commenced. In 2001 unhappy global villagers shattered the New World Order and pulled an illegal U turn on the Bridge to the 21st Century.

Over a decade of Terrorist War, which should have consisted of a swift campaign of annihilation turned into a drawn out, limited objective campaign consisting of nation building and counter insurgency operations in the name of spreading democracy.

This is not a failure of our military; it is a failure of the civilian leadership of the military. It is furthermore a failure of the American people themselves, who elect such ethically and intellectually bankrupt politicians who are only capable of control and utterly incapable of leadership.

The point is that every American should be able to agree, that the United States ought to be politically, economically, and militarily Independent. Every American should also be able to agree that the way to maintain that independence is to ensure the security and survival of the United States.

This means U.S. uni-polar hegemonic overextension rooted in the idealism of democracy, open markets, free trade, human rights, and collective security, along with moral and ethical judgments on the internal affairs of other nations must be consciously put to an end by the American people. If the American people do not do it for themselves, we will be forced to do it from a position of weakness, under terms we do not like, because our commitments have outnumbered our resources.

This means returning to the principles of Washington's Farewell Address via the Structural Realism advanced by Waltz. The structure of the international system has not changed. Changes in the system are distinct from changes of the system[104]. The reason the neo-liberal international order advanced by the United States since 1945 is crumbling all around us whether in Ukraine, Syria, Iraq, Afghanistan, the Eurozone, the IMF, or the U.N.

---

[104] (Waltz K. N., Summer 2000)

is due to the failure of a change **in** the international system becoming a change **of** the international system. The attempts of the United States to use hegemony, collective security agreements, and simultaneously prop up international institutions which are designed to create hierarchy in a system of anarchy have failed.

Whether one likes it or not or whether one admits it or not, the United States is an overextended unipolar hegemon that is headed face first into an anarchic multipolar regional realignment. I submit the following grand strategy to maximize the Independence, Security, and Survival of the United States of America.

The political, economic, and military independence of the United States has to be re-established. In the past our independence was declared from the United Kingdom. Today the United States ought to declare our independence from the rest of the world. Such a thing is obviously difficult, due to the United States promoting complex interdependence since 1945, however in order to maximize our independence, security, and survival it is absolutely necessary and proper.

The liberal international order of complex interdependence advanced by the United States has diminished our political, economic, and military independence by ceding sovereignty to international institutions, ceding economic self determination to international institutions, and enabling international institutions to judge whether our use of military force is acceptable or not. If the primary national interest of the United States is political, economic, and military independence, then the international institutions we helped create no longer serve our interests and ought to be disbanded.

There is a distinct difference between idealistic interests and realistic interests. The United States is approaching 100 years of being guided by Woodrow Wilson's idealistic worldview. The battle to impose hierarchy on anarchy has failed. The battle to make the world safe for democracy has failed. The liberal international order the United States seeks to enforce is crumbling while our independence, security, and survival continues to be diminished each time we seek to impose hierarchy on anarchy.

Chapter 2 International Relations and Foreign Policy

The grand strategy of the United States should be to maximize its Independence, Security, and Survival, which I shall call a grand strategy of Common Defense.

The Constitutional provisions that authorize common defense can be divided into 3 categories: The Production of Military Goods and Services, The Provision of National Defense, and Authorizations to conduct International Relations and Foreign Policy (Appendix 1F).

Given these constitutional authorizations and the anarchic structure of the international system identified by George Washington and Kenneth Waltz, it is appropriate to begin describing how to maximize the political, economic, and military independence of the United States using the constitutional authorizations to conduct international relations and foreign policy.

Conduct of International Relations and Foreign Policy
Article 1 Section 8
To define and punish Piracies and Felonies committed on the high Seas, and Offences against the Law of Nations;

To declare War, grant Letters of Marque and Reprisal, and make Rules concerning Captures on Land and Water;

Article 2 Section 2
He shall have Power, by and with the Advice and Consent of the Senate, to make Treaties, provided two thirds of the Senators present concur;

Congress is granted the authority to define and punish piracies and felonies committed on the high seas as well as offences against the law of nations. Before one gets excited and attempts to justify the United States enforcing United Nations resolutions and International Law under the auspices of "punish offences against the law of nations" let us remember what Madison wrote in Federalist 42. The Articles of Confederation *"contain no provision for the case of offenses against the law of nations; and consequently leave it in the power of any indiscreet member to embroil the Confederacy with foreign nations. The provision of the federal articles on piracies and felonies extends no further than to the establishment of courts for the trail of these offenses*[105]*"*.

Jon Roland, a Libertarian candidate for Attorney General in Texas, compiled a list of the law of nations from Blackstone's Commentaries circa 1788.

"(1) No attacks on foreign nations, their citizens, or shipping, without either a declaration of war or letters of marque and reprisal.

---

[105] (Madison, http://teachingamericanhistory.org/library/document/federalist-no-42/)

(2) Honoring of the flag of truce, peace treaties, and boundary treaties. No entry across national borders without permission of national authorities.

(3) Protection of wrecked ships, their passengers and crew, and their cargo, from depredation by those who might find them.

(4) Prosecution of piracy by whomever might be able to capture the pirates, even if those making the capture or their nations had not been victims.

(5) Care and decent treatment of prisoners of war.

(6) Protection of foreign embassies, ambassadors, and diplomats, and of foreign ships and their passengers, crew, and cargo while in domestic waters or in port.

(7) Honoring of extradition treaties for criminals who committed crimes in a nation with whom one has such a treaty who escape to one's territory or are found on the high seas[106]".

These were the laws of nations as they were understood in 1788. Notice that none of these laws diminish the independence and sovereignty of a nation that observes them. It is also to be noted that the benefits of observing these 7 "agreements" exceed the costs of not observing them. Despite anarchy prevailing in the international system, cooperation, and civil relations are indeed possible and ought to be encouraged.

As the law of nations evolved into more complex agreements and understandings, there

---

[106] (Roland, 1998)

should have been a point at which the United States declined to participate in arrangements that diminished our political, economic, and military independence.

To declare War, grant Letters of Marque and Reprisal, and make Rules concerning Captures on Land and Water;

Congress is granted the authority to declare war. The Common Defense Strategy is submitted in order to minimize the exposure of the United States to war. As the United States increases its political and economic independence, America will increase its military independence.

Letters of marque and reprisal are completely under-utilized in the United States. America is in its 13th year of terrorist war, yet letters of marque and reprisal have not been issued since the War of 1812. The Declaration of Paris in 1856 prohibits privateering however the United States did not ratify the 1856 declaration[107]. If the United States is facing non-state actors that wage war using asymmetric means and terrorism to offset our numerical superiority, superiority of firepower, while exploiting our weakness of adhering to international law and norms, it would give the United States a tremendous advantage to counter our non-state foes using a similar non-state force which is decentralized, unrestricted, and unrestrained.

The failure to issue letters of marque and reprisal is a Congressional failure. The Congress is conditioned to duck and cover behind the War Powers Act. The War Powers Act has its legitimate

---

[107] (Yoo)

applications in a fast moving world, however the failure of Congress to supplement spontaneous military engagements by following through with the ability of non-state actors responding to an asymmetric threat, burdens our military with operations that are not of the highest levels of violence and intensity. The United States military is designed to win high intensity, high violence conflicts. They should not be forced to engage in prolonged low to medium intensity operations that also involve nation building and counterinsurgency campaigns, which they do not enjoy a comparative advantage in waging.

Congress was also granted the authority to make rules concerning captures on land and water. Captures were specifically intended to include enemy property and not enemy personnel. The seizure of enemy property on the battlefield by forces other than the United States military, i.e. non-state actors, executing letters of marque and reprisal, are governed by rules established by Congress[108]. Obviously captures of enemy property made by the United States armed forces are governed by the rules of engagement and the commander's intent. In the cases of enemy property captured by non-state actors executing letters of marque and reprisal, these captures are specifically regulated by Congress.

He shall have Power, by and with the Advice and Consent of the Senate, to make Treaties, provided two thirds of the Senators present concur;

Out of the 3 constitutional clauses which authorize the conduct of international relations and foreign policy the power of the president to make

---

[108] (Yoo, http://www.heritage.org/constitution#!/)

treaties with 2/3 of the senate agreeing is the most powerful, even more powerful than the Congressional power to declare war. The reason being is that the United States can cede political, economic, and military independence on paper in a piecemeal fashion, to an extent that would not even be possible by the loss of war. This is the most troublesome and problematic issue I have with contemporary American grand strategy. The United States is committed to multiple defense treaties, multiple economic agreements, and multiple political compacts that diminish the political, economic, and military independence of the United States.

Treaties that diminish both the political and military independence of the United States are numerous.

27 hot shooting wars are automatically triggered by Article 5 of NATO. The United States via treaty must treat an attack on any of the following nations as it would treat an attack on the homeland: Albania, Belgium, Britain, Bulgaria, Canada, Croatia, Czech Republic, Estonia, Denmark, France, Germany, Greece, Hungary, Iceland, Italy, Latvia, Lithuania, Luxembourg, Netherlands, Norway, Poland, Portugal, Romania, Slovakia, Slovenia, Spain, and Turkey[109].

The United States signed a mutual defense assistance agreement with Israel in 1952 which established a "moral" commitment to Israeli security[110].

---

[109] (NATO)
[110] (Buchanan, 1999, p. 30)

The United States has 37,000 troops deployed in South Korea, which if attacked will trigger a military response[111].

The U.S.-Japan Mutual Security Treaty of 1960 obligates the United States to treat an attack against Japan or its territories, including the disputed Senkakus islands, as dangerous to America's own peace and safety[112].

The United States is obligated by a 1982 communique to give Taiwan access to American defensive weapons. The U.S. has made a moral commitment to Taiwanese security, very similar to the one made to Israel[113].

The United States is obligated to treat any attack on the Philippines as dangerous to U.S. peace and security since 1951 when a mutual security pact was signed[114].

The United States is committed to defend Thailand through the Manila Pact and a 1962 communique that ensures U.S. military commitment[115].

The United States is obligated to come to the defense of Australia, if they are attacked under the ANZUS Pact of 1951. New Zealand was kicked out of the ANZUS agreement in 1985, but the U.S. is still committed to fight for Australia[116].

---

[111] (Buchanan, 1999, p. 31)
[112] (Buchanan, 1999, p. 31)
[113] (Buchanan, 1999, p. 32)
[114] (Buchanan, 1999, p. 32)
[115] (Buchanan, 1999, p. 32)
[116] (Buchanan, 1999, p. 33)

The United States is also obligated to fight up to 21 hot shooting wars through the Treaty of Rio which took effect in 1948. Article 3 of the Treaty of Rio has very similar language to Article 5 of NATO, where an attack against one, will be considered an attack against all. Member nations include Argentina, Bahamas, Bolivia, Brazil, Chile, Columbia, Costa Rica, Dominican Republic, Ecuador, El Salvador, Guatemala, Haiti, Honduras, Mexico, Nicaragua, Panama, Paraguay, Peru, Trinidad and Tobago, Uruguay, and Venezuela[117].

The United States is obligated by treaty, communique, and moral commitment to wage war over 55 countries. Not only do these obligations diminish American political and military independence, the United States does not have the capability to fulfill its commitments. The right of the United States to reserve its neutrality is gone, given our current obligations and commitments. Our inability to reserve neutrality in 55 instances is a clear and significant give away of American political independence and American military independence.

"If we remain one people under an efficient government. the period is not far off when we may defy material injury from external annoyance; when we may take such an attitude as will cause the neutrality we may at any time resolve upon to be scrupulously respected; when belligerent nations, under the impossibility of making acquisitions upon us, will not lightly hazard the giving us provocation; when we may choose peace or war, as our interest, guided by justice, shall counsel[118]."

---

[117] (Buchanan, 1999, p. 33)

[118] (Washington, 1796)

The obligations to these 55 nations all occurred during the course of the Cold War. The failure of the United States to end these obligations at the end of the Cold War directly violates Washington's admonition that *"It is our true policy to steer clear of permanent alliances with any portion of the foreign world[119]"*. These treaties and alliances must be wound down.

NATO should be disbanded. It is time for Europe to defend itself. Europe is perfectly capable of defending itself and should be encouraged to do so. The United States should keep some of our bases in Europe in order to project force. Israel is perfectly capable of defending itself and should be encouraged to. The permanent presence of U.S. troops in South Korea ought to be withdrawn because South Korea is capable of defending itself and should be encouraged to. The United States should keep some of our bases in Japan in order to project force however Japan is capable of defending itself and should be encouraged to do so. The Philippines and Thailand are capable of defending themselves and should be encouraged to do so. Australia is capable of defending itself and should be encouraged to do so. The Treaty of Rio should be disbanded as the nations of the Western Hemisphere are capable of defending themselves and should be encouraged to do so.

These alliances and treaties may have been necessary and proper during the bi-polar struggle between Western Liberalism and Communism during the Cold War, however that struggle ended in 1991. The uni-polar hegemony of the United States

---

[119] (Washington, 1796)

from 1991-2014 that was designed to prevent another great power from rising to challenge the U.S. and to enforce and expand the post WWII liberal international order has left the U.S. overextended and in decline.

U.S. uni-polar hegemony, overextension, and decline are sore subjects for American politicians. American politicians are in denial of American hegemony, overextension, and decline. This is evidenced by the failure of American politicians to either scale back American commitments in line with our resources, or to increase our resources in order to meet our commitments. The denial of the "Lippman Gap" and failure to do anything about it is a sure sign of overextension and decline[120].

It is necessary to identify and examine the causes of decline because the United States is currently facing them in spades!

>"Excessive private consumption (opulence, low savings ratio)
>Excessive public consumption (government overspending)
>Military overextension
>Foreign borrowing that leads to an unfavorable exchange rate
>Loss of technological innovativeness
>Dimunition of risk taking propensity
>Regulatory rigidities that impede efficiency
>Capital outflows that are not recovered
>Manpower shortages: military, civilian labor
>Lower literacy

---

[120] (Dueck, 2013)

Built in limits to growth: environment,
resource, physical space
Declining net new investment
Reduced competiveness regarding market
share[121]"

The United States has engaged in a uni-polar
hegemonic drive to advance a liberal world order
that's goal is to tear down trade barriers and open up
markets. The removal of trade barriers and access to
new markets has actually contracted the production
possibilities frontier of the United States (which was
discussed in Chapter 3). This PPF contraction has
negative consequences for American economic
independence, as well as American political and
military independence.

Given the path of American decline and the
rise of Russia, China, India, and Brazil, the regional
multi-polar realignment is just over the horizon. The
time for action is sooner rather than later, because it
is in the interest of the United States to maximize its
power and shape the multi-polar regional
realignment from a position of strength, instead of
maintaining its denial and having to adjust to a
changing status quo later from a position of
weakness.

*"The international system — as constructed
following the Second World War — will be almost
unrecognizable by 2025. Indeed, "international
system" is a misnomer as it is likely to be more
ramshackle than orderly, its composition hybrid and
heterogeneous as befits a transition that will still be
a work in progress in 2025. The transformation is
being fueled by a globalizing economy, marked by an*

---

[121] (Doran, 1991)

historic shift of relative wealth and economic power from West to East, and by the increasing weight of new players — especially China and India. The US will remain the single most important actor but will be less dominant[122].

Again, the post WWII liberal international order is collapsing because anarchy is inherent in the international system. The uni-polar world in which the United States is hegemonic is also collapsing due the decline caused by the very system we attempted to prop up and prolong. The historic shift of relative wealth and economic power from West to East is caused by the de-industrialization of the United States, policies of free trade, our inability to create an independent energy policy, and a demographic explosion in the developing world.

The constitutional authorizations for conducting international relations and foreign policy can be used to increase American political and military independence by unwinding the treaties that bind us to political and military obligations. The United States can also conduct international relations and foreign policy in a manner that unwinds the international political institutions we created and continue to prop up that diminish our political independence and our sovereignty by withdrawing our support for them because they no longer serve our interests. International relations and foreign policy should also be used to shore up the economic independence of the United States by withdrawing support for the international institutions we created and continue to maintain that have restrained our ability to expand our production possibilities frontier

---

[122] (National Intelligence Council, 2008)

in a significant manner. If political, economic, and military independence are not the primary vital strategic interests of the United States, uni-polar overextension, along with political, economic, and military decline will be accelerated.

Chapter 3 Military Goods and Services and National Defense

The constitution specifically authorizes the production of military goods and services.

Production of Military Goods and Services
Article 1 Section 8
To raise and support Armies, but no Appropriation of Money to that Use shall be for a longer Term than two Years;

To provide and maintain a Navy;

To make Rules for the Government and Regulation of the land and naval Forces;

To provide for organizing, arming, and disciplining, the Militia, and for governing such Part of them as may be employed in the Service of the United States, reserving to the States respectively, the Appointment of the Officers, and the Authority of training the Militia according to the discipline prescribed by Congress;

These 4 clauses are the foundation of the military industrial complex. Obviously raising and supporting Armies while providing and maintain a Navy requires significant industrial production. Vehicles, ships, weapons systems, and equipment do not grow organically, so such items cannot be harvested. Military goods have to be produced in high quantities and be manufactured in a high quality by industrial means. Over time these military goods wear out and need to be replaced. Over time military goods can become obsolete because they are surpassed by new technology. Over time new technology enables new types of military goods to be produced.

Congress was given the authority to raise, support, provide, and maintain the armed forces, govern and regulate them, as well as provide, organize, arm, and discipline the militia.

The extent of the size and influence of industrial sector that produces military goods is a legitimate question to debate, especially when the production of weapons systems is spread out through multiple congressional districts, where varying districts produce various components of one weapons system. The extent of the size and influence of the consulting and information sector that produces military services, such as intelligence, training, doctrine development, information, and logistics are also legitimate questions given the size and scope of their services.

The production of military goods and services requires industrial production as well as production from the consulting and information sectors.

The constitution specifically authorizes the national defense of the United States. In most cases, these clauses establish the militia as a key mechanism to defend against insurrections, rebellions, invasions, imminent danger, and domestic violence.

Provision of National Defense
Article 1 Section 8
To provide for calling forth the Militia to execute the Laws of the Union, suppress Insurrections and repel Invasions;

Section 9
The Privilege of the Writ of Habeas Corpus shall not be suspended, unless when in Cases of Rebellion or Invasion the public Safety may require it.

Section 10
No State shall enter into any Treaty, Alliance, or Confederation; grant Letters of Marque and Reprisal;

No State shall, without the Consent of Congress, lay any Duty of Tonnage, keep Troops, or Ships of War in time of Peace, enter into any Agreement or Compact with another State, or with a foreign Power, or engage in War, unless actually invaded, or in such imminent Danger as will not admit of delay.

Article 2 Section 2
The President shall be Commander in Chief of the Army and Navy of the United States, and of the Militia of the several States, when called into the actual Service of the United States;

Article 4 Section 4
The United States shall guarantee to every State in this Union a Republican Form of Government, and shall protect each of them against Invasion; and on Application of the Legislature, or of the Executive (when the Legislature cannot be convened), against domestic Violence.

Amendment 2
A well-regulated Militia, being necessary to the security of a free State, the right of the people to keep and bear Arms, shall not be infringed.

Amendment 3
No Soldier shall, in time of peace be quartered in any house, without the consent of the Owner, nor in time of war, but in a manner to be prescribed by law.

The militia was designed as a firewall to defend American independence and sovereignty. Given the small size of the American Army and Navy in the late 1780's it was absolutely possible, that an alliance of empires could defeat the American Army and Navy in a short period of time. After the defeat of the standing army and navy, the independence and sovereignty of the United States, our very security and survival as a nation would be on the shoulders of the local *ad hoc* militias.

In contemporary times with technological advances in weaponry such as nuclear missiles, electromagnetic pulse explosions, bio weapons, cyber-attacks designed to disrupt the electrical grid and other critical infrastructure, the capabilities of the armed forces may be so diminished, and the command and control structure may have been vaporized or destroyed. In such a case will the National Guard be unaffected and able to perform its duties, or will its effectiveness be comparably diminished? If the answer is yes, then the *ad hoc* local American militia remains the firewall against insurrections, rebellions, invasions, imminent danger, and domestic violence.

According to U.S. Code Title 10, 311 :
(a) The militia of the United States consists of all able-bodied males at least 17 years of age and, except as provided in section 313 of title 32, under 45 years of age who are, or who have made a declaration of intention to become, citizens of the United States and of female citizens of the United States who are members of the National Guard.

(b) The classes of the militia are —
(1) the organized militia, which consists of the National Guard and the Naval Militia; and
(2) the unorganized militia, which consists of the members of the militia who are not members of the National Guard or the Naval Militia.

In the worst case scenario, where the government of the United States along with all of the armed forces and organized militia are destroyed or incapacitated by nuclear weapons, electromagnetic pulse attacks, cyber-attacks, or bio weapons it is the unorganized militia, all able bodied males from 17-45 years of age who must rise to the occasion and preserve our constitutional republic and way of life.

In another scenario competing for the worst case, where the Federal government, and the governments of the States have become tyrannical and despotic, and the police enforce unconstitutional and illegal laws, and the military has failed to uphold their oath to defend the constitution against domestic enemies, all able bodied males from 17-45 years of age must rise to the occasion to preserve our constitutional republic and way of life.

Another terrible scenario which would require all able bodied males from 17-45 years of age to rise to the occasion and defend the constitutional republic and way of life, would be a collapse of the financial system and economy followed by a collapse of the entire federal system, from the Town, to the County, to the City, to the State, to the Government of the United States itself. It would be left to the unorganized militia to reestablish order, provide public goods and services, uphold the constitution, and schedule new elections.

"There is something so far-fetched and so extravagant in the idea of danger to liberty from the militia that one is at a loss whether to treat it with gravity or with raillery; whether to consider it as a mere trial of skill, like the paradoxes of rhetoricians; as a disingenuous artifice to instil prejudices at any price; or as the serious offspring of political fanaticism. Where in the name of common sense are our fears to end if we may not trust our sons, our brothers, our neighbors, our fellow-citizens? What shadow of danger can there be from men who are daily mingling with the rest of their countrymen and who participate with them in the same feelings, sentiments, habits and interests?[123]"

Danger to liberty is occurring from the national security apparatus constructed post 9/11 to keep the homeland secure for the duration of the terrorist war. Danger to American liberty is found in provisions of the Patriot Act, danger to liberty is inherent in NSA blanket surveillance, and danger to American liberty is inherent in the National Defense Authorization Act of Fiscal year 2012[124].

---

[123] (Hamilton A. , Federalist 29)

[124] (Hamilton A. , Federalist 26) *"Schemes to subvert the liberties of a great community require time to mature them for execution. An army, so large as seriously to menace those*

The liberty/security tradeoff is even more important that the equity/efficiency tradeoff. It is critical that the United States gets both of them right. There needs to be enough security to maximize liberty in order for efficiency to provide the adequate amount of equity within America.

On one hand Hamilton's warnings about the subversion of liberty are sound and timely; on the other hand Hamilton also issued warnings equally as sound and timely about the authorities essential to the common defense. Hamilton argued theses powers ought to exist without limitation[125].

---

liberties, could only be formed by progressive augmentations; which would suppose not merely a temporary combination between the legislature and executive, but a continued conspiracy for a series of time. Is it probable that such a combination would exist at all? Is it probable that it would be persevered in, and transmitted along through all the successive variations in a representative body, which biennial elections would naturally produce in both houses? Is it presumable that every man the instant he took his seat in the national Senate or House of Representatives would commence a traitor to his constituents and to his country? Can it be supposed that there would not be found one man discerning enough to detect so atrocious a conspiracy, or bold or honest enough to apprise his constituents of their danger? If such presumptions can fairly be made, there ought at once to be an end of all delegated authority. The people should resolve to recall all the powers they have heretofore parted with out of their own hands, and to divide themselves into as many States as there are counties in order that they may be able to manage their own concerns in person

[125] (Hamilton A. , Federalist 23) *The authorities essential to the common defense are these: to raise armies; to build and equip fleets; to prescribe rules for the government of both; to direct their operations; to provide for their support. These powers ought to exist without limitation,* because it is impossible to foresee or define the extent and variety of national exigencies, and the correspondent extent and variety of the means which

Hamilton did not have a balance in mind between a national security apparatus formed over time, by progressive augmentations, that seriously menaces liberty, and the powers of common defense existing without limitation. It is clear from the wording of Federalist 26, Hamilton would pull the plug on those in control of the system who enabled the subversion of liberty to occur.

Today the United States has a thriving military industrial complex and a growing national security apparatus which are constitutionally authorized. The national security apparatus creates friction with our Bill of Rights. The size and influence of the military industrial complex is capable of swaying policy makers towards increased military engagements and increased security measures.

Reestablishing our political and military independence through the use of international relations and foreign policy will disentangle the United States from permanent alliances, foreign entanglements, and rigid treaties that do not maximize our independence. This in turn will allow the United States to focus on the requirements of military goods and services and national defense from the standpoint of a multi polar world which has realigned regionally. Uni polar global hegemony

---

may be necessary to satisfy them. *The circumstances that endanger the safety of nations are infinite, and for this reason no constitutional shackles can wisely be imposed on the power to which the care of it is committed. This power ought to be coextensive with all the possible combinations of such circumstances; and ought to be under the direction of the same councils which are appointed to preside over the common defense.*

requires a higher degree of military goods and services and national security output, than does a multi polar power that is the primary force in its hemisphere.

Chapter 4 Common Defense for the Multi Polar Regional Realignment

The multi-polar regional realignment has begun, and during this transitional period between a uni-polar world and a multi-polar world, the United States has to begin to begin conducting itself accordingly.

Using international relations and foreign policy to increase the political and military independence of the United States is fresh in the readers mind. Using international relations and foreign policy to increase the economic independence of the United States by withdrawing from the international institutions we created after WWII such as the IMF, WTO, and WBO is another necessary action. Continued membership in the Bank for International Settlements ought to be considered as a mechanism to resolve currency disputes between the primary economic powers throughout the multi-polar regions.

The grand strategy of Common Defense does not include political, economic, or military isolationism. The core of the grand strategy of Common Defense is political, economic, and military independence. This does not mean an end to the participation of the United States in globalization. It simply means globalization will occur in a regionalized context, and regionalization will be primary, while globalization will be secondary.

The 2 most critical elements of economic independence related to the multi-polar regional realignment will be the development and security of

America's energy resources, and the development and security of a sound American currency backed by gold.

The days of the dollar as the world's reserve currency are obviously numbered. The United States ought to be developing and securing its energy resources and a currency backed by gold immediately, in order to disentangle from international political, economic, and military commitments when the time comes sooner rather than later. If the United States can develop and secure energy resources and develop and secure a sound currency, it will be able to better compete and excel in a regionally realigned multi polar system in which other powers have developed and secured their own energy resources and currencies.

One has to look no further than the East to observe the regional realignment of energy resources and currency alternatives to the dollar being developed by Russia and China. A quick observation of the Middle East will reveal the transfer of gold from Turkey to Iran, the proposed Iranian-Syrian central bank, the proposed Iranian-Syrian pipeline, various other pipelines through the Middle East and South Asia, and competition for the surface minerals of Afghanistan.

One can observe the Shanghai Cooperation Organization whose main goals are *"strengthening mutual confidence and good-neighbourly relations among the member countries; promoting effective cooperation in politics, trade and economy, science and technology, culture as well as education, energy, transportation, tourism, environmental protection and other fields; making joint efforts to maintain and ensure peace, security and stability in the region, moving towards the establishment of a new, democratic, just and rational political and economic international order[126]"*

Member states include: China, Russia, Kazakhstan, Kyrgyz Republic, Tajikistan, and Uzbekistan. Observer states include: Afghanistan, Pakistan, India, Iran, and Mongolia. Dialogue partners include: Belarus, Turkey, and Sri Lanka.

U.S. uni-polar hegemony to advance the post WWII liberal economic order is on is on a collision course with the nations of the Shanghai Cooperation Organization who are *"moving towards the establishment of a new, democratic, just and rational political and economic international order"*. It's not a good idea for the U.S. to overextend itself and hasten its decline fighting against the new political and economic international order attempting to be established by the Shanghai Cooperation Organization.

There is no international order because the structure of the international system is anarchic. The United States should focus on advancing a regional order. In fact the map of the Unified Combatant Commands is a good starting point, to observe what a multi-polar regional realignment looks like.

---

[126] (Shanghai Cooperation Organization)

127

Above is the Department of Defense's Unified Combatant Command structure. This is a good observation of regionalization. The map may have intended to be a uni-polar superpower's view of the world. The map is even more useful for illustrating the multi-polar regional realignment and the grand strategy of common defense.

Brazil, Russia, India, China and South Africa, constitute the BRICS. The BRICS are countries whose economies are expanding. The BRICS are labeled in the next map.

---

127 (DOD)

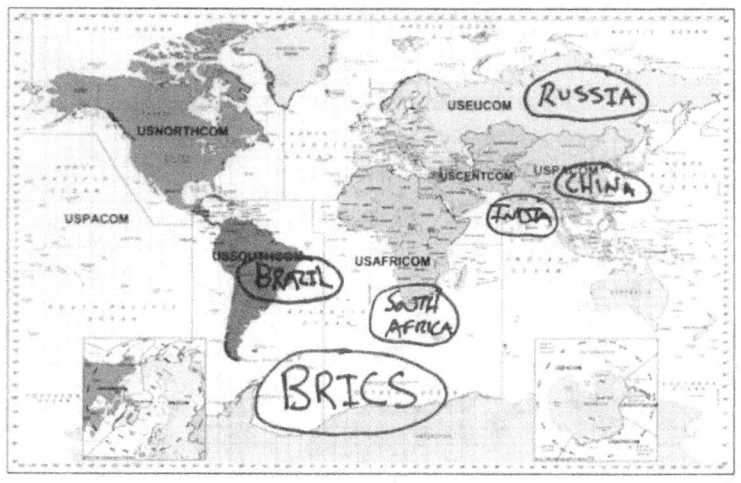

This is a view of the BRICS and the coming multipolar regional realignment. If the United States will use international relations and foreign policy to wind down the 55 defense arrangements we have around the world, as well as develop and secure our energy resources and a currency backed by gold, the United States will become an independent regional superpower.

Each of the BRICS countries will become major powers in each of their regions. The BRICS will be political, economic, and military powers that will be the primary strategic players in each region. In each region there will also be countries the United States is close to politically, economically, and militarily, despite the recent expiration of defensive arrangements. This may serve as a natural balancing within the region. The following map provides some examples.

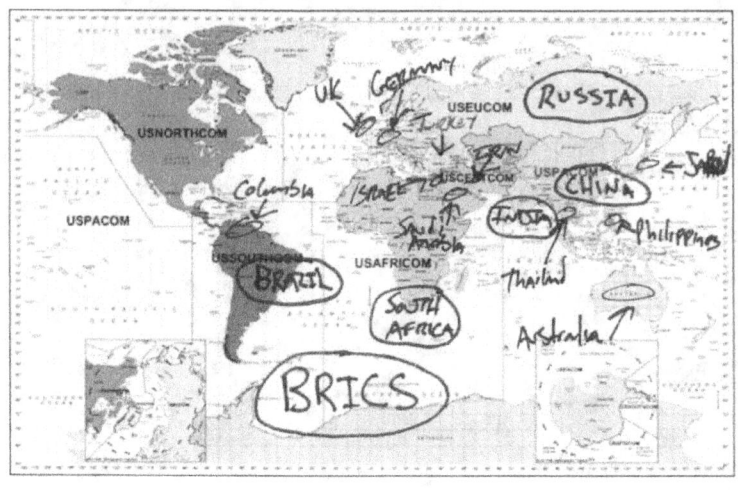

U.S. Pacific Command is a great place to start.

     The regional political, economic, and military powers of this region will be India and China. Japan and Australia are the primary friends of the United States in this region. Thailand, the Philippines, Indonesia, and Malaysia are commercial partners. Commerce in this region could expand rapidly if the energy resources were secured and developed along with sound currencies. U.S. presence and influence in this region has prevented Japan and Australia from taking a greater role in the regions political and economic affairs. The United States does not need to be micromanaging the political, economic, and military affairs of this region. India, China, Japan, Australia and the other countries of the region are perfectly capable of working things out amongst themselves.

Continuing with U.S. European Command.

     The primary political, economic, and military powers of this region will be Russia and the European Union. The primary friends of the United States in this region are the United Kingdom and

171

Germany. There are many commercial partners in this region also. Russia will continue to develop energy, exchange currency, and seek to influence China and the Middle East. A Europe without NATO could develop its own defense force structure, expand its economy, and naturally balance Russia. The United States does not need to be micromanaging the political, economic, and military affairs of this region. Russia, the EU, and Turkey and the other countries in the region are perfectly capable of working things out amongst themselves.

Next is U.S. Central Command.

The primary political, economic and military powers of the region will be Iran, Pakistan, Saudi Arabia, and Israel. Other important regional players include the Gulf States, Jordan, and Egypt. If the United States, India, China, Russia, and the EU can develop and secure their energy resources and establish sound currencies, the geopolitical significance of the Middle East will significantly decline. The primary reason the U.S. deals with the Middle East is due to energy and Israel. Israel is perfectly capable of defending itself. The United States is also perfectly capable of using its own energy resources which is the way out of Middle Eastern ethnic and sectarian civil wars. Israel, Iran, Saudi Arabia, and Pakistan are capable of keeping the status quo in the Mideast.

The U.S. African Command and U.S. Southern Command are next.

These regions have the most to gain by a multi-polar regional realignment. Africa and South America can expand their economies by developing their raw material, agricultural, industrial, and energy assets. Africa and South America will expand their production possibilities frontier's by supplying the resources North America, the EU, Russia, India, and China will consume.

Finally, U.S. Northern Command.

This region is home. Along with Canada, Mexico, and several Caribbean islands this should be the primary focus of the United States. It is here that we defend. It is here that we produce agricultural goods for export. It is here that we produce manufactured goods for export. It is here that we produce energy for ourselves before we sell it on the international market. It is here that we create the soundest currency in the international system. It is here that we secure our borders in accordance with our sovereignty and independence.

If a call to maximize the independence, sovereignty, security, and survival of the United States through strategic disengagement, and strategic multi-polar realignment is categorized as isolationism and weakness, let those who make such accusations explain how uni-polar hegemonic overextension will maximize the independence, sovereignty, security and survival of the United States in the 21st century.

The grand strategy of Common Defense enables the United States to establish operational and tactical solutions that maximize our forces ability to fight and win conflicts at the highest levels of intensity and violence. Common Defense accounts for the principles of combined arms/maneuver warfare and *collapse from within* 4th generation of warfare methods. The use of 3rd and 4th generation warfare enables the United States to engage in expeditionary campaigns of annihilation or limited objective campaigns when our independence, security, survival, and sovereignty are threatened.

The grand strategy of Common Defense is essentially multi-polar regional structural realism. If we take the anarchy inherent in the structure of the international system, and use the recommendations Washington made in his Farewell Address, the United States can navigate the imminent multi-polar regional realignment without significant negative impact.

We must retract the 55 tripwires for war we have set.

We must develop and secure our energy resources and infrastructure.

We must establish a currency backed by gold.

We must secure our borders.

We must make the object of trade the maximization of U.S. benefits.

We must adhere to the sound and timely advice aforementioned from Washington, Hamilton, and Madison.

We must recognize the international system is anarchic. From 1648-1945 the system was multi-polar, from 1945-1991 bipolar, from 1991-2008 it was unipolar, from 2008-Current the international system is in a transition from uni-polar to multi-polar.

We must adhere to the constitutional provisions for: international relations and foreign policy, production of military goods and services, and for national defense.

We must "keep all options on the table" by not making moral, ethical, and emotional arguments for intervening in the internal affairs of foreign nations. This will enable the United States to observe neutrality and participate in Realpolitik when we choose.

We must maximize the political, economic, and military independence of the United States in the 21st century.

Constitutional Capitalism and Common Defense are essential to each other. We must work towards both simultaneously. The expansion of the PPF in a constitutional and independent manner is essential to the security, survival, and independence of the United States. It is the key to a healthy and robust national economy. It is the key to competing in the regional economy. It is required to compete in robust commercial exchange at the global level.

The multi-polar regional realignment shouldn't be considered a defeat for the United States. Having a multi-polar regional realignment does not automatically classify the United States as losers. The United States can maximize the benefits of a multi-polar regional realignment, far beyond any other nation.

Overseas military commitments drastically reduced,

The military industrial complex and national security apparatus significantly reduced,

Political, economic, and military independence maximized,

The independence, security and survival of the United States maximized throughout the 21st Century.

Part III

Appendix 1

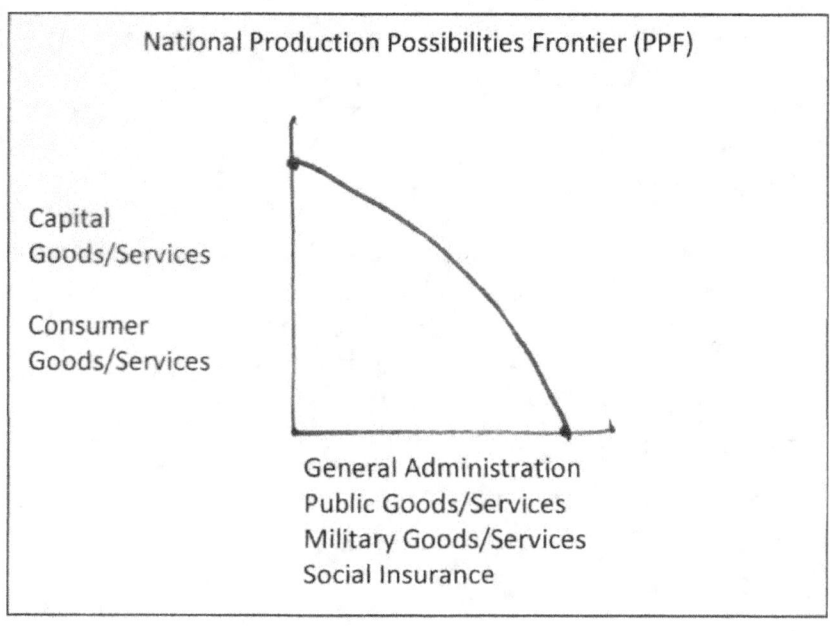

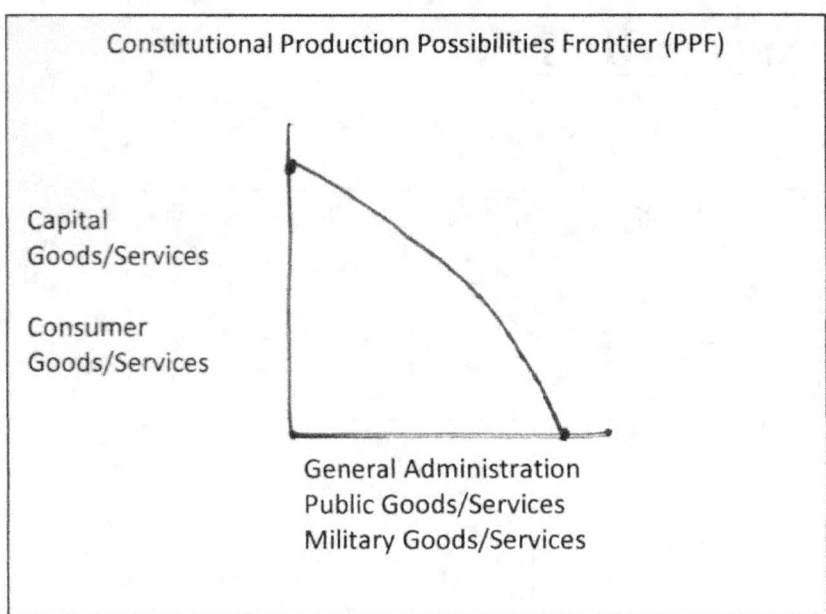

Constitutional Production Possibilities Frontier (PPF)

Capital
Goods/Services

Consumer
Goods/Services

General Administration
Public Goods/Services
Military Goods/Services

Trade Offs and Opportunity Costs

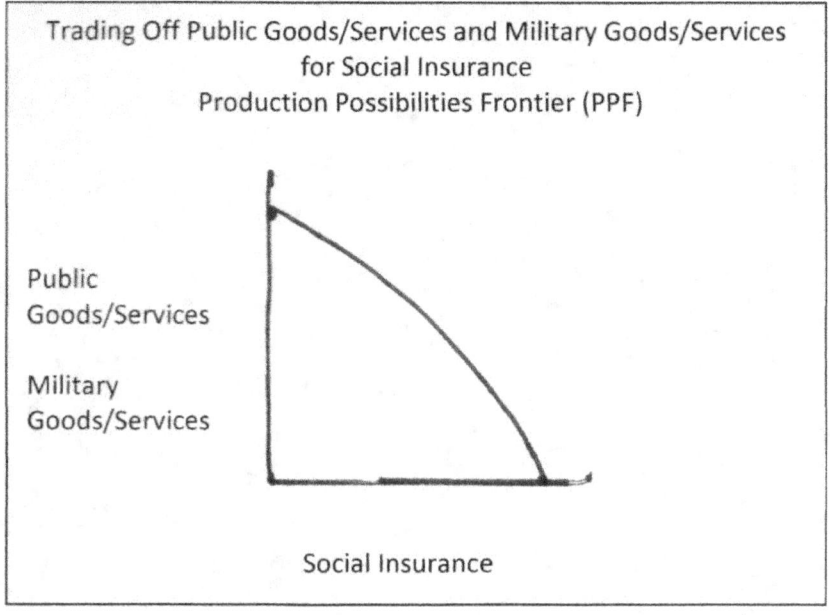

Trading Off Public Goods/Services and Military Goods/Services
for Social Insurance
Production Possibilities Frontier (PPF)

Public
Goods/Services

Military
Goods/Services

Social Insurance

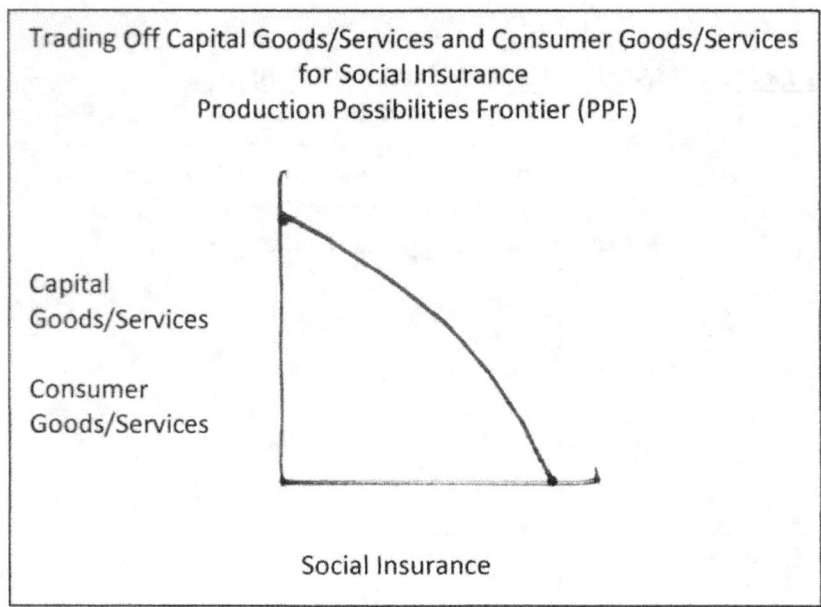

Trading Off Capital Goods/Services and Consumer Goods/Services
for Social Insurance
Production Possibilities Frontier (PPF)

Capital
Goods/Services

Consumer
Goods/Services

Social Insurance

The States

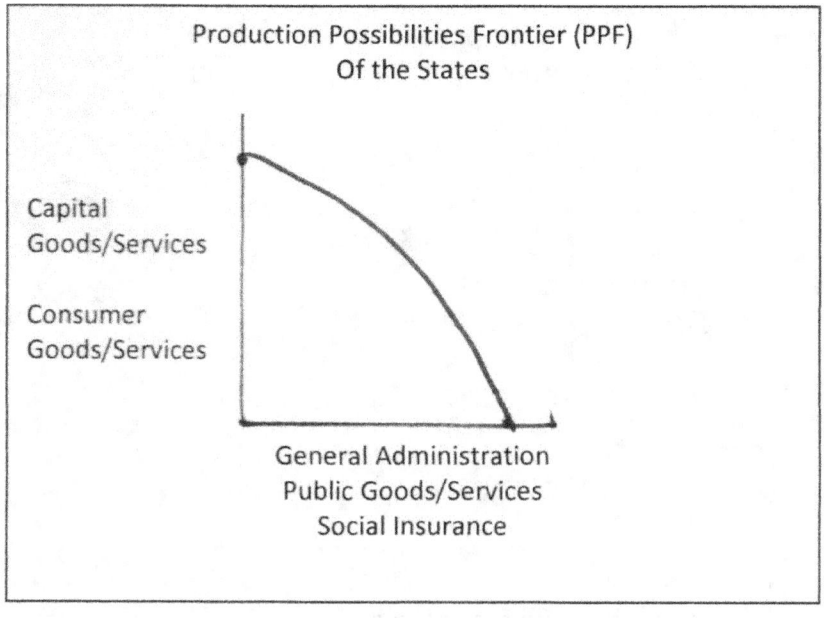

Local Governments and Municipalities

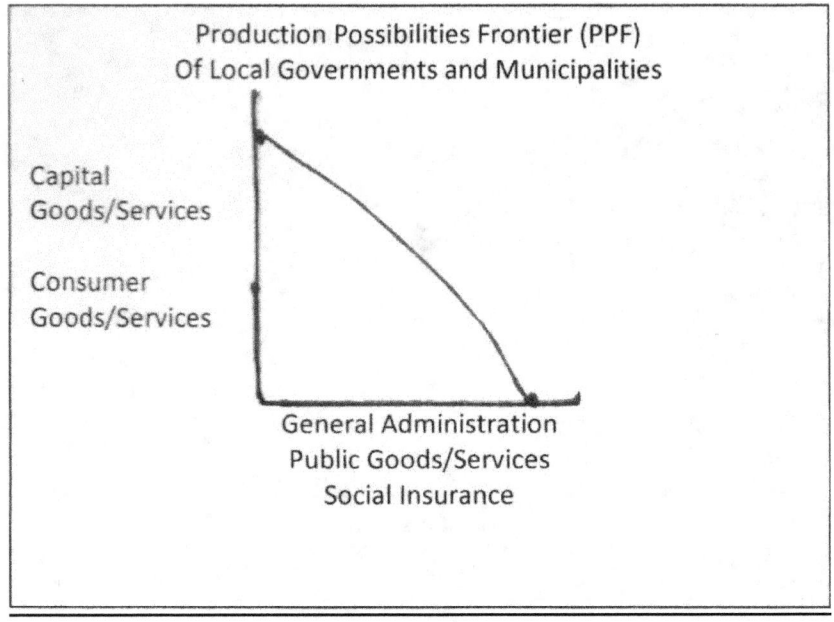

The Same Trade Offs and Opportunity Costs at the State, Local, and Municipal Levels

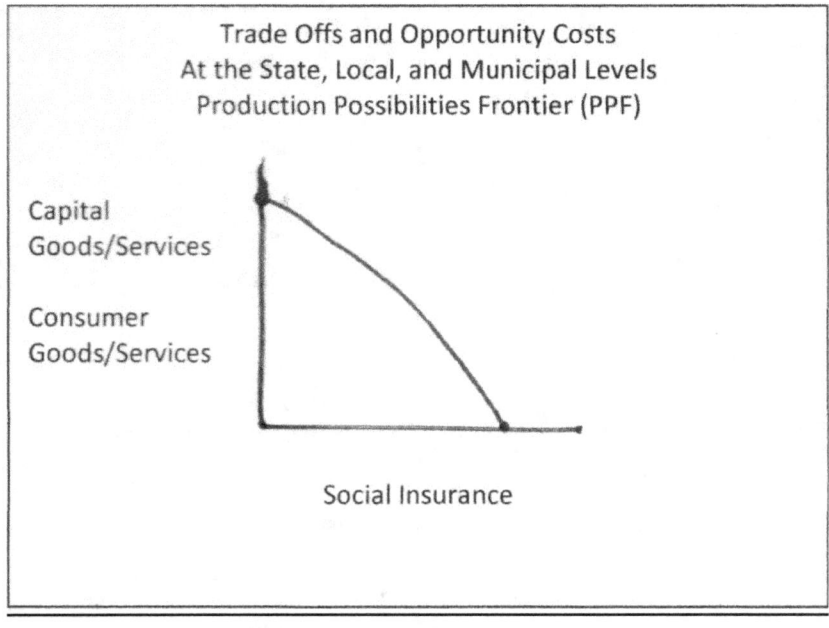

Trade Offs and Opportunity Costs
At the State, Local, and Municipal Levels
Production Possibilities Frontier (PPF)

Capital Goods/Services

Consumer Goods/Services

Social Insurance

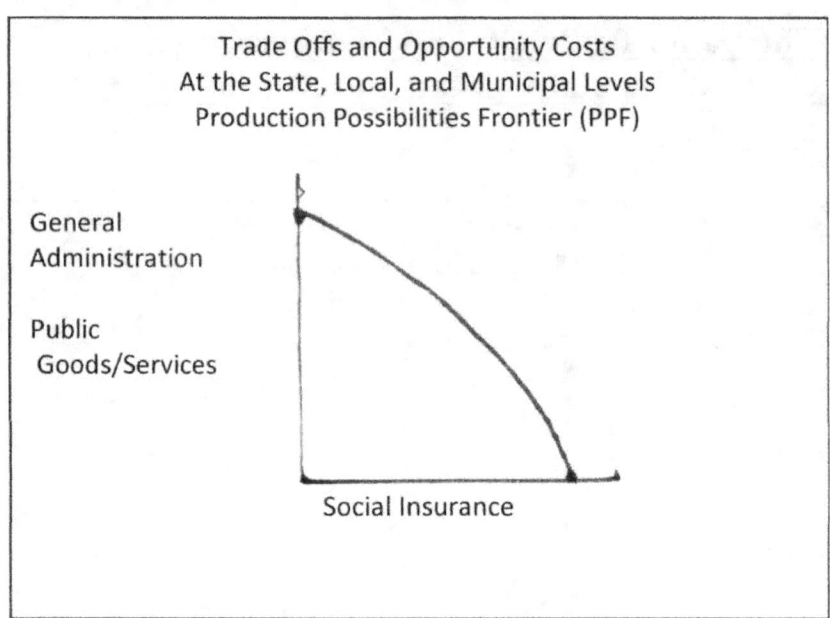

Trade Offs and Opportunity Costs
At the State, Local, and Municipal Levels
Production Possibilities Frontier (PPF)

General
Administration

Public
Goods/Services

Social Insurance

Appendix 1A

General Economic Rules
Article 1
Section 8
To regulate commerce with foreign nations, and among the several states, and with the Indian tribes;
To establish a uniform rule of naturalization, and uniform laws on the subject of bankruptcies throughout the United States;

Section 9
The migration or importation of such persons as any of the states now existing shall think proper to admit, shall not be prohibited by the Congress prior to the year one thousand eight hundred and eight, but a tax or duty may be imposed on such importation, not exceeding ten dollars for each person.
No tax or duty shall be laid on articles exported from any state.
No preference shall be given by any regulation of commerce or revenue to the ports of one state over those of another: nor shall vessels bound to, or from, one state, be obliged to enter, clear or pay duties in another.

Article 2
Section 2
He shall have Power, by and with the Advice and Consent of the Senate, to make Treaties, provided two thirds of the Senators present concur;

Fiscal Policy
Article 1
Section 7
All bills for raising revenue shall originate in the House of Representatives; but the Senate may propose or concur with amendments as on other Bills.

Section 8
The Congress shall have power to lay and collect taxes, duties, imposts and excises, to pay the debts and provide for the common defense and general welfare of the United States; but all duties, imposts and excises shall be uniform throughout the United States;
To borrow money on the credit of the United States;
To make all laws which shall be necessary and proper for carrying into execution the foregoing powers, and all other powers vested by this Constitution in the government of the United States, or in any department or officer thereof.

Section 9
No money shall be drawn from the treasury, but in consequence of appropriations made by law; and a regular statement and account of receipts and expenditures of all public money shall be published from time to time.

Section 10
No state shall, without the consent of the Congress, lay any imposts or duties on imports or exports, except what may be absolutely necessary for executing it's inspection laws: and the net produce of all duties and imposts, laid by any state on imports or exports, shall be for the use of the treasury of the United States; and all such laws shall be subject to the revision and control of the Congress.

No state shall, without the consent of Congress, lay any duty of tonnage

Article 6
All debts contracted and engagements entered into, before the adoption of this Constitution, shall be as valid against the United States under this Constitution, as under the Confederation.

14th Amendment Section 4
The validity of the public debt of the United States, authorized by law, including debts incurred for payment of pensions and bounties for services in suppressing insurrection or rebellion, shall not be questioned. But neither the United States nor any state shall assume or pay any debt or obligation incurred in aid of insurrection or rebellion against the United States, or any claim for the loss or emancipation of any slave; but all such debts, obligations and claims shall be held illegal and void.

16th Amendment
The Congress shall have power to lay and collect taxes on incomes, from whatever source derived, without apportionment among the several states, and without regard to any census or enumeration.

Monetary Policy
Article 1
Section 8
to pay the debts and provide for the common defense and general welfare of the United States
To borrow money on the credit of the United States;
To coin money, regulate the value thereof, and of foreign coin, and fix the standard of weights and measures;

To provide for the punishment of counterfeiting the securities and current coin of the United States;

Section 9
No money shall be drawn from the treasury, but in consequence of appropriations made by law; and a regular statement and account of receipts and expenditures of all public money shall be published from time to time.

Section 10
No state shall….. coin money; emit bills of credit; make anything but gold and silver coin a tender in payment of debts;

Article 6
All debts contracted and engagements entered into, before the adoption of this Constitution, shall be as valid against the United States under this Constitution, as under the Confederation.

14th Amendment Section 4
The validity of the public debt of the United States, authorized by law, including debts incurred for payment of pensions and bounties for services in suppressing insurrection or rebellion, shall not be questioned. But neither the United States nor any state shall assume or pay any debt or obligation incurred in aid of insurrection or rebellion against the United States, or any claim for the loss or emancipation of any slave; but all such debts, obligations and claims shall be held illegal and void.

Compensation
Article 1 Section 6
The Senators and Representatives shall receive a compensation for their services, to be ascertained by law, and paid out of the treasury of the United States.

Article 2 Section 1
The President shall, at stated times, receive for his services, a compensation, which shall neither be increased nor diminished during the period for which he shall have been elected, and he shall not receive within that period any other emolument from the United States, or any of them.

Article 3 Section 1
The judges, both of the supreme and inferior courts, shall hold their offices during good behavior, and shall, at stated times, receive for their services, a compensation, which shall not be diminished during their continuance in office.

27th Amendment
No law, varying the compensation for the services of the Senators and Representatives, shall take effect, until an election of Representatives shall have intervened.

Regulations on Executive and Judicial Branches
Article 2 Section 3
He shall from time to time give to the Congress information of the state of the union, and recommend to their consideration such measures as he shall judge necessary and expedient;

Article 3 Section 2
The judicial power shall extend to all cases, in law and equity, arising under this Constitution, the laws of the United States,

Regulations on the States
Article 1
Section 10
No state shall enter into any treaty, alliance, or confederation; grant letters of marque and reprisal; coin money; emit bills of credit; make anything but gold and silver coin a tender in payment of debts; pass any bill of attainder, ex post facto law, or law impairing the obligation of contracts, or grant any title of nobility.
No state shall, without the consent of the Congress, lay any imposts or duties on imports or exports, except what may be absolutely necessary for executing it's inspection laws: and the net produce of all duties and imposts, laid by any state on imports or exports, shall be for the use of the treasury of the United States; and all such laws shall be subject to the revision and control of the Congress.
No state shall, without the consent of Congress, lay any duty of tonnage, keep troops, or ships of war in time of peace, enter into any agreement or compact with another state, or with a foreign power, or engage in war, unless actually invaded, or in such imminent danger as will not admit of delay.

21st Amendment Section 1
The eighteenth article of amendment to the Constitution of the United States is hereby repealed.

Section 2
The transportation or importation into any state, territory, or possession of the United States for delivery

or use therein of intoxicating liquors, in violation of the laws thereof, is hereby prohibited.

24th Amendment Section 1
The right of citizens of the United States to vote in any primary or other election for President or Vice President, for electors for President or Vice President, or for Senator or Representative in Congress, shall not be denied or abridged by the United States or any state by reason of failure to pay any poll tax or other tax.

Decentralization to the States
9th Amendment
The enumeration in the Constitution, of certain rights, shall not be construed to deny or disparage others retained by the people.

10th Amendment
The powers not delegated to the United States by the Constitution, nor prohibited by it to the states, are reserved to the states respectively, or to the people.

Prohibition of Slavery
13th Amendment
Neither slavery nor involuntary servitude, except as a punishment for crime whereof the party shall have been duly convicted, shall exist within the United States, or any place subject to their jurisdiction.

Appendix 1B

Constitutional Authorizations for Public Goods/Services
Article 1
Section 8

To establish post offices and post roads;

To promote the progress of science and useful arts, by securing for limited times to authors and inventors the exclusive right to their respective writings and discoveries;

To coin money, regulate the value thereof, and of foreign coin, and fix the standard of weights and measures;

To provide for the punishment of counterfeiting the securities and current coin of the United States;

To exercise exclusive legislation in all cases whatsoever, over such District (not exceeding ten miles square) as may, by cession of particular states, and the acceptance of Congress, become the seat of the government of the United States, and to exercise like authority over all places purchased by the consent of the legislature of the state in which the same shall be, for the erection of forts, magazines, arsenals, dockyards, and other needful buildings;--And

To make all laws which shall be necessary and proper for carrying into execution the foregoing powers, and all other powers vested by this Constitution in the government of the United States, or in any department or officer thereof.

To regulate commerce with foreign nations, and among the several states, and with the Indian tribes;

To establish a uniform rule of naturalization, and uniform laws on the subject of bankruptcies throughout the United States;

Section 9

The migration or importation of such persons as any of the states now existing shall think proper to admit, shall not be prohibited by the Congress prior to the year one thousand eight hundred and eight, but a tax or duty may be imposed on such importation, not exceeding ten dollars for each person.

Article 3

Section 1

The judges, both of the supreme and inferior courts, shall hold their offices during good behavior, and shall, at stated times, receive for their services, a compensation, which shall not be diminished during their continuance in office.

Section 2

The judicial power shall extend to all cases, in law and equity, arising under this Constitution, the laws of the United States,

10th Amendment

The powers not delegated to the United States by the Constitution, nor prohibited by it to the states, are reserved to the states respectively, or to the people.

Appendix 1C

Military Goods/Services Authorized

Article 1
Section 8

To define and punish Piracies and Felonies committed on the high Seas, and Offences against the Law of Nations;

To declare War, grant Letters of Marque and Reprisal, and make Rules concerning Captures on Land and Water;

To raise and support Armies, but no Appropriation of Money to that Use shall be for a longer Term than two Years;

To provide and maintain a Navy;

To make Rules for the Government and Regulation of the land and naval Forces;

To provide for calling forth the Militia to execute the Laws of the Union, suppress Insurrections and repel Invasions;

To provide for organizing, arming, and disciplining, the Militia, and for governing such Part of them as may be employed in the Service of the United States, reserving to the States respectively, the Appointment of the Officers, and the Authority of training the Militia according to the discipline prescribed by Congress;

Section 9

The Privilege of the Writ of Habeas Corpus shall not be suspended, unless when in Cases of
Rebellion or Invasion the public Safety may require it.

Section 10
No State shall enter into any Treaty, Alliance, or Confederation; grant Letters of Marque and Reprisal; No State shall, without the Consent of Congress, lay any Duty of Tonnage, keep Troops, or Ships of War in time of Peace, enter into any Agreement or Compact with another State, or with a foreign Power, or engage in War, unless actually invaded, or in such imminent Danger as will not admit of delay.

Article 2
Section 2
The President shall be Commander in Chief of the Army and Navy of the United States, and of the Militia of the several States, when called into the actual Service of the United States;
He shall have Power, by and with the Advice and Consent of the Senate, to make Treaties, provided two thirds of the Senators present concur;

Article 4
Section 4
The United States shall guarantee to every State in this Union a Republican Form of Government, and shall protect each of them against Invasion; and on Application of the Legislature, or of the Executive (when the Legislature cannot be convened), against domestic Violence.

Amendment 2
A well-regulated Militia, being necessary to the security of a free State, the right of the people to keep and bear Arms, shall not be infringed.

Amendment 3

No Soldier shall, in time of peace be quartered in any house, without the consent of the Owner, nor in time of war, but in a manner to be prescribed by law.

Appendix 1D

Constitutional Authorization for Fiscal Policy

Article 1
Section 7
All bills for raising revenue shall originate in the House of Representatives; but the Senate may propose or concur with amendments as on other Bills.

Section 8
The Congress shall have power to lay and collect taxes, duties, imposts and excises, to pay the debts and provide for the common defense and general welfare of the United States; but all duties, imposts and excises shall be uniform throughout the United States;
To borrow money on the credit of the United States;
To make all laws which shall be necessary and proper for carrying into execution the foregoing powers, and all other powers vested by this Constitution in the government of the United States, or in any department or officer thereof.

Section 9
No money shall be drawn from the treasury, but in consequence of appropriations made by law; and a regular statement and account of receipts and expenditures of all public money shall be published from time to time.

Section 10
No state shall, without the consent of the Congress, lay any imposts or duties on imports or exports, except what may be absolutely necessary for executing it's inspection laws: and the net produce of all duties and

imposts, laid by any state on imports or exports, shall be for the use of the treasury of the United States; and all such laws shall be subject to the revision and control of the Congress.
No state shall, without the consent of Congress, lay any duty of tonnage

Article 6
All debts contracted and engagements entered into, before the adoption of this Constitution, shall be as valid against the United States under this Constitution, as under the Confederation.

14th Amendment Section 4

The validity of the public debt of the United States, authorized by law, including debts incurred for payment of pensions and bounties for services in suppressing insurrection or rebellion, shall not be questioned. But neither the United States nor any state shall assume or pay any debt or obligation incurred in aid of insurrection or rebellion against the United States, or any claim for the loss or emancipation of any slave; but all such debts, obligations and claims shall be held illegal and void.

16th Amendment
The Congress shall have power to lay and collect taxes on incomes, from whatever source derived, without apportionment among the several states, and without regard to any census or enumeration.

Appendix 1E

Constitutional Authorization for Monetary Policy

Article 1
Section 8
To pay the debts and provide for the common defense and general welfare of the United States
To borrow money on the credit of the United States;
To coin money, regulate the value thereof, and of foreign coin, and fix the standard of weights and measures;
To provide for the punishment of counterfeiting the securities and current coin of the United States;

Section 9
No money shall be drawn from the treasury, but in consequence of appropriations made by law; and a regular statement and account of receipts and expenditures of all public money shall be published from time to time.

Section 10
No state shall..... coin money; emit bills of credit; make anything but gold and silver coin a tender in payment of debts;

Article 6
All debts contracted and engagements entered into, before the adoption of this Constitution, shall be as valid against the United States under this Constitution, as under the Confederation.

14th Amendment Section 4

The validity of the public debt of the United States, authorized by law, including debts incurred for payment of pensions and bounties for services in suppressing insurrection or rebellion, shall not be questioned. But neither the United States nor any state shall assume or pay any debt or obligation incurred in aid of insurrection or rebellion against the United States, or any claim for the loss or emancipation of any slave; but all such debts, obligations and claims shall be held illegal and void.

Appendix 1F

Production of Military Goods and Services

Article 1 Section 8
To raise and support Armies, but no Appropriation of Money to that Use shall be for a longer Term than two Years;
To provide and maintain a Navy;
To make Rules for the Government and Regulation of the land and naval Forces;
To provide for organizing, arming, and disciplining, the Militia, and for governing such Part of them as may be employed in the Service of the United States, reserving to the States respectively, the Appointment of the Officers, and the Authority of training the Militia according to the discipline prescribed by Congress;

Provision of National Defense
Article 1 Section 8
To provide for calling forth the Militia to execute the Laws of the Union, suppress Insurrections and repel Invasions;

Section 9
The Privilege of the Writ of Habeas Corpus shall not be suspended, unless when in Cases of
Rebellion or Invasion the public Safety may require it.

Section 10
No State shall enter into any Treaty, Alliance, or Confederation; grant Letters of Marque and Reprisal;

No State shall, without the Consent of Congress, lay any Duty of Tonnage, keep Troops, or Ships of War in time of Peace, enter into any Agreement or Compact with another State, or with a foreign Power, or engage in

War, unless actually invaded, or in such imminent Danger as will not admit of delay.

Article 2 Section 2
The President shall be Commander in Chief of the Army and Navy of the United States, and of the Militia of the several States, when called into the actual Service of the United States;

Article 4 Section 4
The United States shall guarantee to every State in this Union a Republican Form of Government, and shall protect each of them against Invasion; and on Application of the Legislature, or of the Executive (when the Legislature cannot be convened), against domestic Violence.

Amendment 2
A well-regulated Militia, being necessary to the security of a free State, the right of the people to keep and bear Arms, shall not be infringed.

Amendment 3
No Soldier shall, in time of peace be quartered in any house, without the consent of the Owner, nor in time of war, but in a manner to be prescribed by law.

Conduct of International Relations and Foreign Policy
Article 1 Section 8
To define and punish Piracies and Felonies committed on the high Seas, and Offences against the Law of Nations;

To declare War, grant Letters of Marque and Reprisal, and make Rules concerning Captures on Land and Water;

Article 2 Section 2

He shall have Power, by and with the Advice and Consent of the Senate, to make Treaties, provided two thirds of the Senators present concur;

Acknowledgments

Thanks be to God and the Holy Spirit, whose guidance and inspiration manifested themselves in the plastic Jesus I purchased on E-Bay that is perched on the filing system on my desk which oversaw the writing process.

Thanks to Charles Tibedo for his knowledge, critical thinking, objectivity, and friendship. His support and encouragement for this project, as well as his honest and constructive feedback were essential to the completion of this project.

Thanks to Michelle Newton, my soul mate, my love. Your support, encouragement, and love made clicking away on the keyboard through many long nights bearable. While writing through the night into the dawn, traveling through the wilderness of academic economic wasteland, traveling through the theoretical and ideological wasteland of uni-polar overextension, I never once felt isolated or alone. I always knew you'd be on the other side to greet me with a warm smile when I returned. Thank you so much. I love you always.

Works Cited

Buchanan, P. (1999). *A Republic Not an Empire.* Washington D.C.: Regnery.

Bureau of Labor Statistics. (n.d.). *http://data.bls.gov/timeseries/LNS11300000.* Retrieved from http://data.bls.gov/timeseries/LNS11300000: http://data.bls.gov/timeseries/LNS11300000

California State University, Northridge. (n.d.). Retrieved from http://www.google.com/url?sa=t&rct=j&q=&esrc=s&source=web&cd=11&cad=rja&uact=8&ved=0CCYQFjAAOAo&url=http%3A%2F%2Fwww.csun.edu%2F~hceco008%2Fc24ci-jm.doc&ei=pOc4U4KHJcmqsQSZioFw&usg=AFQjCNGLLb8g0lgMf1ohiqprLlvtd0tTMw&sig2=2U0AYoCJvIjcXwxMqvUP7A&bvm=bv.6380

Conant, M. (1974). *The Constitution and Capitalism.* St. Paul: West Publishing Co.

DOD. (n.d.). Retrieved from http://www.defense.gov/ucc/

Doran, C. (1991). *Systems In Crisis.* New York: Cambridge University Press.

Dueck, C. (2013, March 27). *Obama's Strategic Denial.* Retrieved from http://nationalinterest.org: http://nationalinterest.org/commentary/obamas-strategic-denial-8275

econport.org. (n.d.). *econport.org.* Retrieved from econport.org: http://www.econport.org/content/handbook/NatIncAccount/CalculatingGDP/Income.html

Federal Reserve Bank of St. Louis. (n.d.). *https://research.stlouisfed.org/fred2/categories/21.* Retrieved from https://research.stlouisfed.org/fred2/categories/21: https://research.stlouisfed.org/fred2/categories/21

Federal Reserve Statistical Release H.4.1. (n.d.). *http://www.federalreserve.gov/releases/h41/current/.* Retrieved from http://www.federalreserve.gov/releases/h41/current/: http://www.federalreserve.gov/releases/h41/current/

Forbes, S. (2005). *Flat Tax Revolution.* Washington D.C.: Regnery.

Government Accountability Office. (n.d.).
*http://www.gao.gov/fiscal_outlook/understanding_fed
eral_debt/overview#t=0*. Retrieved from
http://www.gao.gov/fiscal_outlook/understanding_fe
deral_debt/overview#t=0:
http://www.gao.gov/fiscal_outlook/understanding_fe
deral_debt/overview#t=0

Grant, S. B. (2007). *The Evolution of Economic Though.* Mason:
SouthWest Cengage.

Gruber, J. (2011). *Public Finance and Public Policy.* New York:
Worth Publishers.

Hamilton, A. (1790). Report on a National Bank. In R. Morris,
Alexander Hamilton and the Founding of the Nation
(pp. 349-350). New York: The Dial Press 1957.

Hamilton, A. (n.d.). *Federalist 23*. Retrieved from
http://teachingamericanhistory.org/library/document/
federalist-no-23/:
http://teachingamericanhistory.org/library/document/
federalist-no-23/

Hamilton, A. (n.d.). *Federalist 26*. Retrieved from
http://teachingamericanhistory.org/library/document/
federalist-no-26/:
http://teachingamericanhistory.org/library/document/
federalist-no-26/

Hamilton, A. (n.d.). *Federalist 29*. Retrieved from
http://teachingamericanhistory.org/library/document/
federalist-no-29/:
http://teachingamericanhistory.org/library/document/
federalist-no-29/

Hamilton, A. (n.d.).
*http://teachingamericanhistory.org/library/document/
federalist-no-33/*. Retrieved from
http://teachingamericanhistory.org/library/document/
federalist-no-33/:
http://teachingamericanhistory.org/library/document/
federalist-no-33/

Hamilton, M. J. (1787). *Federalist Papers.*

Howard, B. K. (2013, January Labor Force Participation and
Work Status of People 65 Years and Older).
*http://www.census.gov/prod/2013pubs/acsbr11-
09.pdf*. Retrieved from

http://www.census.gov/prod/2013pubs/acsbr11-09.pdf:
http://www.census.gov/prod/2013pubs/acsbr11-09.pdf

List of great powers by date. (n.d.). Retrieved from
http://en.wikipedia.org/wiki/Great_power

List of pre-modern great powers. (n.d.). Retrieved from
http://en.wikipedia.org/wiki/List_of_pre-modern_great_powers

Luttwak, E. (1987). *Strategy: The Logic of War and Peace.*
Cambridge: Belknap Harvard.

Madison, J. (n.d.).
*http://teachingamericanhistory.org/library/document/
federalist-no-10/.* Retrieved from
http://teachingamericanhistory.org/library/document/
federalist-no-10/:
http://teachingamericanhistory.org/library/document/
federalist-no-10/

Madison, J. (n.d.).
*http://teachingamericanhistory.org/library/document/
federalist-no-42/.* Retrieved from
http://teachingamericanhistory.org/library/document/
federalist-no-42/:
http://teachingamericanhistory.org/library/document/
federalist-no-42/

Madison, J. (n.d.).
*http://teachingamericanhistory.org/library/document/
federalist-no-44/.* Retrieved from
http://teachingamericanhistory.org/library/document/
federalist-no-44/:
http://teachingamericanhistory.org/library/document/
federalist-no-44/

Madison, J. (n.d.).
*http://teachingamericanhistory.org/library/document/
federalist-no-44/.* Retrieved from
http://teachingamericanhistory.org/library/document/
federalist-no-44/:
http://teachingamericanhistory.org/library/document/
federalist-no-44/

Malone, C. C. (2010). *Public Policy.* Boulder: Lynne Rienner.

McEachern, W. (2009). *Microeconomics.* Mason: South Western Cengage.

merriam-webster.com. (n.d.). Retrieved from merriam-webster.com: http://www.merriam-webster.com/dictionary/inequity

merriam-webster.com. (n.d.). *merriam-webster.com.* Retrieved from http://www.merriam-webster.com/dictionary/inequality

merriam-webster.com. (n.d.). *merriam-webster.com.* Retrieved from merriam-webster.com: http://www.merriam-webster.com/dictionary/independence

multpl.com. (n.d.). *www.multpl.com/.* Retrieved from http://www.multpl.com/united-states-population/table

Nalewaik, J. J. (2010, April 15). *http://www.bea.gov.* Retrieved from http://www.bea.gov/about/pdf/nalwaik_gdpvsgdi.pdf: http://www.bea.gov/about/pdf/nalwaik_gdpvsgdi.pdf

National Intelligence Council. (2008, November). *Global Trends 2025: A Transformed World.* Retrieved from http://www.dni.gov/files/documents/Newsroom/Reports%20and%20Pubs/2025_Global_Trends_Final_Report.pdf: http://www.dni.gov/files/documents/Newsroom/Reports%20and%20Pubs/2025_Global_Trends_Final_Report.pdf

NATO. (n.d.). *Allied Command Operations.* Retrieved from NATO: http://www.aco.nato.int/page13615743.aspx

Ray, J. K. (2011). *Global Politics.* Boston: Wadsworth Cengage.

Ricardo, D. (2007). Works and Correspondence. In S. B. Grant, *The Evolution of Economic Thought.* Mason: South Western Cengage.

Roland, J. (1998, The meaning of "Offenses against the Law of Nations"). *http://www.constitution.org/cmt/law_of_nations.htm.* Retrieved from http://www.constitution.org: http://www.constitution.org/cmt/law_of_nations.htm

Schiller, B. R. (2009). *Essentials of Economics.* New York: McGraw-Hill Irwin.

Shanghai Cooperation Organization. (n.d.). *http://www.sectsco.org/EN123/brief.asp.* Retrieved

from http://www.sectsco.org/EN123/brief.asp:
http://www.sectsco.org/EN123/brief.asp

Silfer, S. C. (1992). *The Atlas of Economic Indicators.* New York:
Harper Collins.

Smith, A. (1776). *The Wealth of Nations.* New York: Bantam
Classic.

The Federal Reserve System. (2005). *Purposes and Functions.*
Washington D.C.: Board of Governors of the Federal
Reserve System .

U.S. Mint. (n.d.). *http://www.usmint.gov/mint_tours/.*
Retrieved from http://www.usmint.gov/mint_tours/:
http://www.usmint.gov/mint_tours/

U.S. Treasury Resource Center. (n.d.).
*http://www.treasury.gov/resource-center/data-chart-
center/tic/Documents/mfh.txt.* Retrieved from
http://www.treasury.gov/resource-center/data-chart-
center/tic/Documents/mfh.txt:
http://www.treasury.gov/resource-center/data-chart-
center/tic/Documents/mfh.txt

Waltz, K. (1979). *Theory of International Politics.* Long Grove:
Waveland Press.

Waltz, K. N. (Summer 2000). Structural Realism After the Cold
War. *International Security*, 5-41.

Washington, G. (1796). *Washington's Farewell Address.*
Retrieved from www.gpo.go:
http://www.gpo.gov/fdsys/pkg/GPO-CDOC-
106sdoc21/pdf/GPO-CDOC-106sdoc21.pdf

www.merriam-webster.com. (n.d.). *http://www.merriam-
webster.com/dictionary/immigration.* Retrieved from
http://www.merriam-
webster.com/dictionary/immigration:
http://www.merriam-
webster.com/dictionary/immigration

www.merriam-webster.com. (n.d.). *http://www.merriam-
webster.com/dictionary/naturalization?show=0&t=139
6755651.* Retrieved from http://www.merriam-
webster.com/dictionary/naturalization?show=0&t=139
6755651: http://www.merriam-
webster.com/dictionary/naturalization?show=0&t=139
6755651

Yoo, J. (n.d.). *http://www.heritage.org/constitution#!/.*
　　　Retrieved from
　　　http://www.heritage.org/constitution#!/articles/1/ess
　　　ays/51/captures-clause
Yoo, J. (n.d.). *www.heritage.org/constitution#!/.* Retrieved
　　　from
　　　http://www.heritage.org/constitution#!/articles/1/ess
　　　ays/50/marque-and-reprisal

Index

I

Immigration
91
Independence
31, 39, 46, 48-9, 51-2, 58, 60, 62-3, 89-98, 109, 114-8, 121, 126-76
Inefficient
26, 33
Inequalities
39-40, 63, 98
Inequality
21, 34-39, 52, 55, 81, 95, 115, 121
Inflation
23, 64, 66, 70-3, 82-3
Intensity
137, 146, 173
International Relations
19, 50, 126, 128, 131-2, 142, 146, 153, 163, 166, 170, 174, 207

J

Jay, John
135
Judicial Precedence
20-1, 25, 29, 35-6, 39, 41, 35, 108, 111, 113-5

L

Limited Objective Campaign
138, 173-4

M

Madison, James
97, 105-6, 135, 143, 174
Maneuver Warfare
173
Market Failure
21, 33-40, 52, 55, 63, 81, 94, 115, 121
Mercantilism
50, 57-8
Mercantilist
50, 57-8, 61-2
Militia
19, 156-161, 198-9, 206-7
Military Goods and Services
4, 16, 18-24, 34-7, 59, 65, 76, 78, 82, 88, 97, 114-9, 142, 156-7, 164, 175, 206
Military Industrial Complex
156, 163, 175
Monetary Policy
16-23, 29-30, 52, 62, 64, 67, 73-4, 81-6, 98, 103, 108-117, 204

www.ingramcontent.com/pod-product-compliance
Lightning Source LLC
Chambersburg PA
CBHW060247290526
45789CB00001B/227